Warman's
Gas Station
Collectibles

Mobiloil
Outboard

TRADE MARKS REG. U.S. PAT. OFF. BY
SOCONY MOBIL OIL COMPANY, INC.

Mark F. Moran

Identification and Price Guide

©2005 Krause Publications
Published by

kp books
An Imprint of F+W Publications

700 East State Street • Iola, WI 54990-0001
715-445-2214 • 888-457-2873

Our toll-free number to place an order or obtain
a free catalog is (800) 258-0929.

Library of Congress Catalog Number: 2005904958

ISBN: 0-89689-162-3

Designed by Kay Sanders
Edited by Dennis Thornton

Printed in China

CONTENTS

Oil Be Seeing You

To see Rich Gannon's eyes light up, do one of the following:

A.) Talk knowledgeably about passing routes, defensive sets and clock management.

B.) Sing the University of Delaware fight song while wearing a Fightin' Blue Hens T-shirt.

C.) Reminisce about your favorite Gulf Oil single-sided tin sign that rates 9.5.

If you answered A or B, you might get a glimmer, but if you answered C, chances are you would also get a personal invitation to visit Gannon's Garage.

Gannon, the 2002 NFL Most Valuable Player as the starting quarterback for the Oakland Raiders, devotes much of his free time to tracking down the best vintage oil and gas advertising he can find. (He also has an extensive collection of soft-drink memorabilia.)

Drafted in the fourth round from the University of Delaware by the New England Patriots in 1987, he was soon traded to the Minnesota Vikings, and maintains close ties to the region.

It's no surprise that many NFL rookies invest in a nice set of wheels as tangible proof of their success. Gannon also had plans to get a special vehicle, but not the kind you might expect.

"My brother liked old cars, so after my rookie year (with the Vikings) in 1987, I went back to Philadelphia (his hometown) and bought this 1960 Buick convertible for $4,400," Gannon recalled, while offering a tour of his converted storage building in suburban Minneapolis. "We spent about two years restoring it, doing the paint, interior, worked on the motor, new top, new tires.

"Then every year at the end of the season, instead of spending $100,000 on a fancy new car, I was buying these old cars. And at one point, I had nine cars, and nowhere to keep them. So I bought this building." Formerly owned by a beer distributor, the brick building has large overhead doors and high ceilings.

"I had these empty, white walls," Gannon said, "so I bought my first sign (advertising Buick Lubricare, with neon).

The interior of Rich Gannon's storage building in suburban Minneapolis is a colorful testament to his love of vintage cars and petroliana.

Oakland Raiders quarterback Rich Gannon holds one of his favorite signs, a single-sided tin example for Sealed Power Piston Rings, which measures 22" by 35", $500+

Three signs in Rich Gannon's collection: Rajah Motor Oil, with surface crazing typical of this sign, 20" by 28", $350; Majestic Batteries, 26" by 19", $400+; Champion Spark Plus, 29 1/2" by 14", $300+.

The walls are no longer empty, but the process required a certain learning curve familiar to all beginning collectors.

As he found out more about collecting, and read magazines about petroliana, Gannon benefited from the experience of advanced collectors.

"I can't tell you how many times, in the beginning, I would be at a show and have something in my hand, and felt like I had a great buy, only to learn it was a reproduction," Gannon recalled with a laugh.

His storage facility now boasts "Gannon's Service": A full-size Gulf gas station, complete with pumps, signs, working restroom, and counter with cash register, maps, and ephemera.

Gannon's eagerness to share his collecting experience grew out of the generosity of other collectors.

"For anyone who's just starting out in the hobby, most collectors are really approachable, and genuine, and happy to help," Gannon said.

His advice?

"Look for examples that are colorful, have great graphics, and are in the best condition. Buy quality, and that means condition, because even if you feel you are paying more than you'd like, the market will catch up with you."

And, he adds, widen your scope, once you've gained knowledge.

"Variety is important. It's fine to focus on globes, but there are so many great signs, cans, paper items, and you can see how different pieces relate to each other."

Words of Thanks

This guide would not have been possible without the help and good wishes of the following folks:
Jane Aumann of Aumann Auctions Inc.
Rich Gannon
George Simpson of Rochester, Minn.
John Hudson

How to Use This Book

This book is organized by form, then alphabetically by firm or manufacturer, and includes sections on containers (tin, glass, cardboard and fiber); displays, holder and racks of all kinds; gas globes; pumps for both oil and gas; signs; other items that don't fall into any of the main categories, and "related" collectibles — often automotive in nature — that appeal to petroliana collectors but are not directly tied to the production of oil and gasoline, like tires, spark plugs, etc., and transportation in general.

Every collecting area has its own language that presents a challenge for beginners. Aumann Auctions Inc., of Nokomis, Ill., a dominant force in the selling of petroliana, uses a number system, primarily to describe the condition of signs and containers. This system ranges from 10 (new in the box) to 1 (a total loss), but most pieces generally fall into the range of 5 (bad) to 9.5 (near mint). These numbers are established by considering the condition of labels, paint and porcelain, scratches, dents, chipping, extra holes, normal and excessive wear, fading, bending and warping. Add to this the factors that determine desirability, such as

graphic impact, rarity and regional collecting tastes, and you can see how difficult it might be for a group of collectors to be unanimous in their assessment of a given piece of petroliana.

For instance, even a category 8 description (considered good condition) assumes significant—or at least noticeable—wear or damage.

Because not all sellers use a similar numbering system, and since opinions about value can vary—sometimes widely—from collector to collector, we have adapted the number system to the following descriptions that are used by enthusiasts in almost all collecting areas:

9.5 — near mint; 9 — excellent; 8.5 — very good; 8 — good; 7.5 — fair to good; 7 — fair; 6.5 — poor to fair; 6 — poor; 5.5 — very poor; 5 — bad.

In the area of petroliana signs, a group of abbreviations is often used:

SSP — Single-Sided Porcelain (sign); PPP — Porcelain Pump Plate; DSP — Double-Sided Porcelain (sign); SST — Single-Sided Tin (sign).

Pricing

The prices in this book have been established using the resources in large, private collections, and with the help of respected dealers and auctioneers. Some petroliana collectors have seen dramatic fluctuations in values over the last decade (usually upward, in this collecting area), but a growing number of reproductions have eroded collector confidence, sending prices for certain vintage pieces lower. And like any investment, collections are subject to changes in the wider economy, and to changing tastes.

When comparing your pieces to examples in this book, pay close attention to details including surface wear, rarity and, of course, cracks and chips, all of which can affect value dramatically.

Many prices in this book also include a "+" sign, which indicates that the value may have been established at an auction, and does not include a buyer's premium, usually 10 percent.

Remember: A price guide not only measures value, but it also captures a moment in time, and sometimes that moment can pass very quickly. The old adage, "An antique is worth what someone will pay for it," is just as true for petroliana as for other collecting areas of longer standing. By using this book and other reliable resources, collectors will learn how to get the best examples for their investment.

Reproductions

There is almost no area of antique collecting that is not plagued by fakes and reproductions. For collectors of vintage gas and oil items, the only way to avoid reproductions is experience: Making mistakes and learning from them; talking with other collectors and dealers; finding reputable resources (including books and Web sites), and learning to invest wisely, buying the best examples one can afford.

Beginning collectors will soon learn that marks can be deceiving, paper labels and tags are often missing, and those that remain may be spurious.

How does one know whether a given piece is authentic? Does it look old, and to what degree can age be simulated? What is the difference between high-quality vintage advertising and modern mass-produced examples? Even experts are fooled when trying to assess qualities that have subtle distinctions.

There is another important factor to consider. A contemporary maker may create a "reproduction" sign or gas globe in tribute of the original, and sell it for what it is: a legitimate copy. Many of these are dated and signed by the artist or manufacturer, and these legitimate copies are highly collectible today. Such items are not intended to be frauds.

But a contemporary piece may pass through many hands between the time it leaves the maker and winds up in a collection. When profit is the only motive of a reseller, details about origin, ownership and age can become a slippery slope of guesses, attribution and—unfortunately—fabrication.

As the collector's eye sharpens, and the approach to inspecting and assessing petroliana improves, it will become easier to buy with confidence. And a knowledgeable collecting public should be the goal of all sellers, if for no other reason than the willingness to invest in quality.

Fortunately, there are entire Web pages devoted to petroliana reproductions. A check of these resources is advised for beginning collectors.

For a wide-ranging look at the many kinds of reproductions in the marketplace, visit www.Repronews.com.

Repronews.com is the online database of fakes and reproductions. It began in 1992 as the monthly printed newsletter, Antique & Collectors Reproduction News. After more than 12 years of producing the black-and-white printed edition, the full-color database was launched in December 2004.

The online database includes all the past articles plus continuous updates on the latest fakes and reproductions as they are discovered. At the time of launch, the database included almost 1,000 articles and reports with more than 7,000 photos and illustrations. Additional research material is also included such as patents from various foreign countries and an extensive marks library.

Articles are searchable with standard search engine techniques, and can also be browsed by title with an A-to-Z list. Subscribers may print articles for personal use on their home or office computers. Color photos and illustrations will print in color on color printers.

Articles are researched and prepared by repronews.com staff in consultation with leading collectors, dealers, clubs and institutions.

The monthly newsletter was begun by publisher Mark Chervenka, who continues to manage the online database.

Resources

Aumann Auctions Inc., 20114 IL Route 16, Nokomis, IL 62075, (888) 282-8648, http://www.aumannauctions.com/

Iola Old Car Show and Swap Meet, P.O. Box 1, Iola, WI 54945, (715) 445-4000, http://www.iolaoldcarshow.com/

Iowa Gas, the nation's largest petroleum and automobile advertising and collectible event, http://www.iowagas.com/main.html

Primarily Petroliana, a community bringing gas station antique collectors, dealers, publishers and service providers together for the benefit of all, http://www.oldgas.com/index.html

Mass Gas Bash, New England's largest gas and oil collectibles swap meet; Mass Gas Collectors Association, P.O. Box 9, East Templeton, MA 01538, http://www.mass-gas-bash.com/index.shtml

Ball Auction Service, 1501 Highway 18 N., Chandler, OK 74834, (405) 258-1511, http://www.ballauctionservice.com/

Maloney's Antiques & Collectibles Resource Directory: Since its debut, Maloney's Antiques & Collectibles Resource Directory has been hailed as the "... best one-volume research tool in print" (Gannett News Service) and as a Best Reference Book (Library Journal), http://www.maloneysonline.com/

Resources listed in Maloney's include:
* Buyers
* Collector Reference Book Sources
* Collectors
* Dealers
* Experts
* General Line and Specialty Auction Services
* Internet Resources
* Manufacturers and Distributors of Modern Collectibles
* Matching Services for China/Flatware/Crystal
* Overseas Antiques Tour Guides
* Regional Guides to Antiques Shops and Flea Markets
* Repair, Restoration and Conservation Specialists
* Reproduction Sources
* Specialty Collector Clubs
* Specialty Museums and Library Collections
* Specialty Periodicals
* Suppliers of Parts
* Trained Appraisers

Containers

Petroliana containers are prized by many collectors. Unlike signs and globes, these were meant to be discarded after use, so they fall into the category of ephemera.

Every collecting area has its own language that presents a challenge for beginners. Aumann Auctions Inc., of Nokomis, Ill., a dominant force in the selling of petroliana, uses a number system, primarily to describe the condition of signs and containers. This system ranges from 10 (new in the box) to 1 (a total loss), but most pieces generally fall into the range of 5 (bad) to 9.5 (near mint). These numbers are established by considering the condition of labels, paint and porcelain, scratches, dents, chipping, extra holes, normal and excessive wear, fading, bending and warping. Add to this the factors that determine desirability, like graphic impact, rarity and regional collecting tastes, and you can see how difficult it might be for a group of collectors to be unanimous in their assessment of a given piece of petroliana.

Because not all sellers use a similar numbering system, and since opinions about value can vary—sometimes widely—from collector to collector, we are using the following descriptions that are used by enthusiasts in almost all collecting areas: near mint, excellent, very good, good, fair to good, fair, poor to fair, poor, very poor and bad.

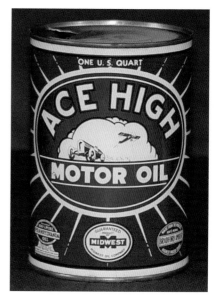

Ace High Motor Oil
quart tin can, near mint.

$875+

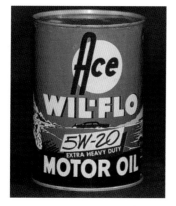

Ace Wil-Flo Motor Oil
quart tin can, excellent condition, small dents around top.

$175+

Aero Eastern Motor Oil
quart tin can, near mint.

$175+

Aero Eastern Motor Oil
two-gallon tin can, fair to good condition, has been welded on.

$60+

Aero Motor Oil
quart tin can, near mint.

$120+

Aero Motor Oil
two-gallon tin can, good condition, has wear.

$50+

Anchor Heavy Duty Motor Oil
tin quart, excellent condition, full.

$140+

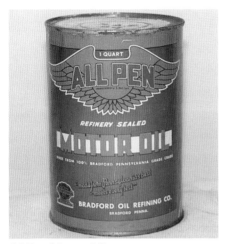

All Pen Motor Oil
tin quart, excellent condition, surface rust around rim.

$50+

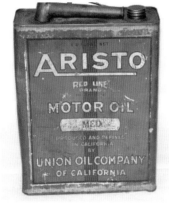

All Pen and XL-Penn Motor Oil
quart tin cans, one fair to good condition, one excellent.

$130+ pair

Air Race Motor Oil Deep-Rock
quart tin can, fair to good condition, worn.

$175+

Archer and Conoco Outboard Motor Oil
tin quarts, both good condition, dents and wear.

$60+ pair

Aristo Motor Oil
one-gallon tin, fair to good condition, dent in back.

$250+

Aristo Motor Oil
1/2-gallon can, poor condition, wear and rust.

$70+

Three assorted
quart tin cans, good to excellent condition.

$10+ all

Three assorted fiber
quart cans, good to excellent condition.

$30+ all

Three assorted
quart tin cans, excellent condition.

$35+ all

Three assorted
quart fiber and tin cans, excellent condition.

$35+ all

Four assorted
quart tin cans, good to excellent condition.

$40+ all

Four assorted
quart tin cans, good condition.

$25+ all

Four assorted
quart tin cans, excellent condition.

$40+ all

Four assorted
quart tin cans, excellent condition.

$75+ all

Five assorted
quart tin cans, including snowmobile, excellent condition.

$30+ all

Five assorted
quart tin cans, excellent condition.

$80+ all

Six assorted motorcycle
quart fiber cans, most good condition.

$40+ all

Six assorted fiber
quart cans, excellent condition.

$30+ all

Six assorted
quart tin cans, good to excellent condition.

$50+ all

Seven assorted
tin and fiber quart cans, most good condition.

$50+ all

Eight assorted fiber
quart cans, very good condition.

$25+ all

Atlantic Motor Oil
Medium one-gallon tin can, light overall wear.

$90+

Five aviation
motor oil quart tin cans, good condition.

$45+ all

Babolene Motor
one-gallon flat tin can, display side excellent,
reverse good, worn.

$500+

Barnsdall tin can
with picture of first refinery, very good condition,
small dent, minor paint loss, full.

$75+

Barnsdall Motor Oil
quart tin can, excellent condition.

$80+

Barnsdall and Golden Shell
quart tin cans, both good condition.

$80+ pair

Bisonoil Motor Oil
quart tin can, near mint.

$300+

Blakely Special Heavy Duty Motor Oil
quart tin can, near mint, small dents.

$550+

Two BSA Motorcycle Oil
quart tin cans, one excellent, one fair to good.

$100+ pair

Calol Engine Oil 8
five-gallon square tin can, Standard Oil (California), display side very good condition, reverse very poor.

$10+

Calol Castor Machine Oil
five-gallon square tin can, Standard Oil (California), with bear logo, paper label fair to good condition.

$20+

Calol Liquid Gloss Absorbing Mop
Standard Oil of California, in round tin can.

$55+

Calol Liquid Gloss
one-pint flat tin can, Standard Oil of California, excellent condition.

$70+

Calol Liquid Gloss
one-quart flat tin can, Standard Oil of California, very good condition, light wear.

$25+

Calol Liquid Gloss
one-gallon flat tin can, Standard Oil of California, very good condition, light wear and dent.

$15+

Calumet Gas Engine Oil
Standard Oil Co., one-gallon square tin can, with Indian, fair to good condition.

$375+

C.A.M. (Indian Motorcycle)
quart tin can, good condition.

$200+

Carter Extra and Humble Bayou City Motor Oil
tin quarts, both good condition.

$90+ pair

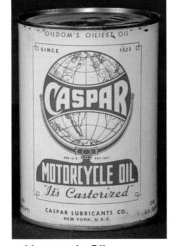

Caspar Motorcycle Oil
quart tin can, excellent condition.

$350+

Three Chevron Starting Fluid
cans and one Ban-Ice can, all excellent condition.

$40+ all

Chief-Penn Motor Oil
two-gallon tin can, good condition.

$110+

Cross-Country Motor Oil
two-quart pitcher, excellent condition.

$75+

Cross-Country Motor Oil
one-gallon flat tin can, sold by Sears, display side excellent, reverse poor, heavy wear.

$225+

Cruiser Motor Oil
quart tin can, near mint.

$200+

Cycol Motor Oil
one-gallon tin can, fair condition.

$140+

Cycol Motor Oil
and New Cycol Motor Oil tin quarts, good condition, some wear.

$275+ pair

Dee-Gumm Vapor Action
quart tin can, excellent condition.

$35+

Derby Super-X
Flex-Lube and Triumph tin quarts, all fair condition.

$375+ all

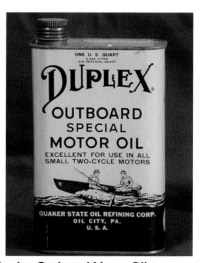

Duplex Outboard Motor Oil
flat quart, near mint.

$60+

Duplex Marine Engine Oil
tin quart, good condition, small dents and wear.

$80+

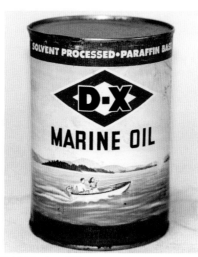

D-X Marine Oil
tin quart, fair to good condition, large dents, full.

$200+

Economy Motor Oil
Wilshire Oil Co., tin quart, excellent condition-plus.

$275+

Elreco Fleet Motor Oil
quart tin can, excellent condition, wear on reverse.
$150+

En-Ar-Co
five-gallon rocker can, both sides fair to good condition.
$150+

Two En-Ar-Co
quart tin cans, excellent condition.
$25+ pair

En-Ar-Co Penn and Regular
quart tin cans, both very good condition.
$75+ pair

Eight En-Ar-Co Oil
one-quart tin cans, good condition or less.
$110+ all

Esso Aquaglide and Marine Oil
tin quarts, good and fair condition, respectively.
$50+ pair

Eureka Belt Dressing
one-pound grease can, Standard (California), very good condition, small dents.
$20+

Eureka Harness Oil
one-gallon square tin can, Standard Oil, worn, fair condition, no dents.
$30+

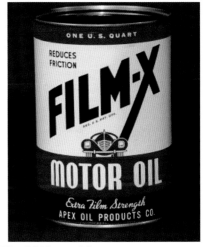

Film-X Motor Oil
quart tin can, near mint.
$80+

Fleet-Wing Certified
tin quarts, good condition.

$70+ pair

Fleetwood Aero Craft Motor Oil
quart tin can, very good condition, has blemish in display and light rust around bottom.

$400+

Ford Anti-Freeze
one-gallon flat tin can, very good condition.

$150+

Fox Head Motor Oil
quart tin can, near mint.

$50+

Frontier-Beeline Antifreeze
one-gallon tin can, excellent condition, minor wear.

$40+

Frontier Econo Lube Motor Oil
quart tin cans, excellent condition.

$50+ pair

Frontier Heavy Duty Motor Oil
quart tin can, near mint, small scratch on reverse.

$175+

Frontier Lube Motor Oil
quart tin can, excellent condition, light wear on reverse.

$250+

Frontier Strato Motor Oil
quart tin can, excellent condition.

$30+

Frontier Ultra Lube Motor Oil
quart tin can, excellent condition.

$35+

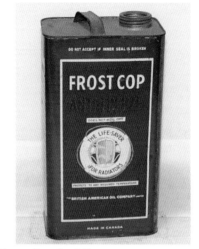

Frontier Ultra Lube Motor Oil
quart tin can, excellent condition, light wear.

$225+

Frost Cop Anti-Freeze
tall Imperial gallon tin, fair to good condition.

$275+

Gebhart's Gold Comet
quart tin can, near mint.

$80+

GEM
quart tin can, excellent condition.

$90+

Two generic oil bottles
one with Mobiloil spout.

$50+ pair

Gilmore
35-pound square grease can, poor to fair condition.

$375+

Gilmore Lion Head
"Purest Premium" tin quart, poor to fair condition, no top or bottom, dents and wear.

$275+

Gilmore Lion Head
"Purest Pennsylvania" tin quart, very good condition, dents and minor wear, full.

$475+

Gilmore Lion Head
"Monarch of Oil" tin quart, excellent condition, some wear.

$275+

Globe Anti-Freeze
one-gallon tin can, excellent condition.

$20+

Golden Leaf Motor Oil
quart tin can, near mint.

$35+

Golden Penn
tin quart can, excellent condition, open on bottom.

$300+

Golden Shell
tin quart, good condition, has some wear.

$30+

Golden West Motor Oil
quart tin can, light wear.

$125+

Grand Penn
and Evercool Motor Oil tin quarts, both good condition, some wear.

$120+ pair

Four graphic
fiber quart cans, good condition.

$60+ all

Green Spot Motor Oil
(General Petroleum) five-gallon square tin can, very good condition.

$250+

Griffin's
Greenzoil and Hyvis Motor Oil tin quarts, all fair to good condition.

$60+ all

Hancock Golden Scot Motor Oil
tin quart, very good condition, small dents.

$80+

Hancock Motor Oil
quart tin can, near mint.

$20+

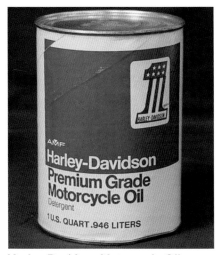

Harley-Davidson Motorcycle Oil
quart cardboard can, excellent condition.

$25+

Harley-Davidson Genuine Oil
one-gallon flat tin can, very good to excellent condition, light wear.

$2,600+

Harley-Davidson Motorcycle Motor Oil
quart tin can with black background, excellent condition, small dents.

$200+

Harley-Davidson Motorcycle Motor Oil
quart tin can with white background, very good condition, light wear and paint checking at bottom.

$250+

Harley-Davidson Motorcycle Motor Oil
quart fiber can, excellent condition.

$30+

Harley-Davidson Motorcycle
five-gallon rocker can, poor to fair condition, overall wear, paint drips on reverse.

$2,250+

Harley-Davidson Motorcycle Motor Oil
Pre-Luxe quart tin can, near mint.

$120+

Harley-Davidson Pre-Luxe
quart tin can, excellent condition-plus, small dent at top.

$150+

Harley-Davidson Pre-Luxe
four pack of quart tin can, with packaging, excellent condition.

$1,300+ set

Harley-Davidson Two-Cycle Motor Oil
12-ounce can, excellent condition.

$100+

Harley-Davidson Motorcycle Two-Cycle Oil
1/2-pint tin can, excellent condition, light wear and dents.

$110+

Harley-Davidson Two-Cycle Motor Oil
four pack of 12-ounce cans, with packaging, all excellent condition.

$1,450+ set

Harris Motor Oil
quart fiber can, excellent condition.

$40+

Harris Motor Oil
and Thermo Anti-Freeze quart tin cans, both good condition.

$80+ pair

Havoline Wax Free
and Havoline Heavy Duty Motor Oil tin quarts, good condition, one full.

$40+ pair

Heccolene
one-pound grease can, very good condition.

$50+

Hermoil Castor Oil Blend
tin quart, excellent condition, small dents.

$160+

Hi-Temp
Tri-State and Wl Superlube Motor Oil tin quarts, all fair to good condition.

$160+ all

HI-VAL-UE Motor Oil
tin quart, very good condition, small dents and minor wear.

$130+

Home
Fedlube and Golden Leaf Motor Oil tin quarts, all good condition.

$50+ all

Hudson Motor Oil
quart jar, very good condition, sealed.

$85+

Hudson Motor Oil
quart tin can, near mint.

$400+

Hudson Motor Oil
quart tin can, near mint.

$325+

Hudson's Pennvein
motor oil quart jar, good condition.

$110+

Hudson Triple A-1
motor oil quart jar, good condition.

$70+

Hudson's Triple L
motor oil quart jar, good condition.

$80+

Husky
one-quart tin oil can, display fair to good condition, reverse bad, full.

$175+

Husky Heavy Duty Motor Oil
quart tin can, orange background, excellent condition, small dents.

$825+

Husky Motor Oil
quart tin can, fair to good condition, has crease and wear.

$575+

Husky Heavy Duty Motor Oil
quart tin can, yellow background, excellent condition, small dents.

$575+

Husky Heavy Duty Motor Oil
quart tin can, front fair condition, reverse poor.

$70+

Husky S-3
and Heavy Duty quart fiber cans, excellent condition.

$25 pair

Husky Superlube
and H/D Lube quart fiber cans, excellent condition.

$25 pair

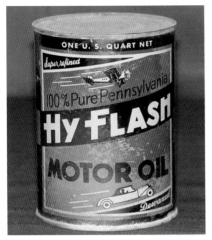

Hy Flash Motor Oil
quart tin can, fair to good condition, fading and
wear.
$375+

HyVis Motor Oil
one-gallon tin, display side good condition, reverse
very poor.
$400+

HyVis
and two different Esso quart tin cans, good condition.
$30+ all

Indian Motorcycle Oil
quart tin can, excellent condition, dent on reverse.
$300+

Indian Motorcycle Oil
quart tin can, very good condition, worn, bottom
out, dented.
$350+

Indian Oil
Valvoline Oil Company one-gallon flat tin can,
excellent condition, light wear.
$4,800+

International Oil Co.
Capitol Hand Separator Oil, half gallon, good
condition.
$40+

Two Invader
and a Sinclair Opaline quart tin cans, all good
condition.
$150+ all

ISO-VIS/Standard
bottle with spout, good condition.
$75+

ISO-VIS
quart oil bottle with grade indicator.

$50+

Kendall
Phillips 66 Aviation and En-Ar-Co quart tin cans, all good condition.

$100+ all

Kendall
and Penn Triumph motor oil quarts, good condition.

$40+ pair

Four Lion
fiber quart cans, excellent condition.

$15+ all

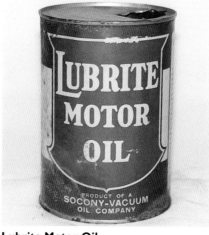

Lubrite Motor Oil
tin quart, Socony, fair condition, faded, wear and small dent.

$40+

Lubrite
and Amalie motor oil quart jars, good condition.

$40+ pair

Magnolia
one-gallon oilcan, paper label, excellent condition.

$400+

Marine Special
and BrayGo Outboard Motor Oil tin quarts, both very good condition.

$80+ pair

Master Outboard Motor Oil
quart tin can, very good condition, light wear.

$550+

McColl Frontenac
embossed one-quart oil bottle, with Indian head.
$280+

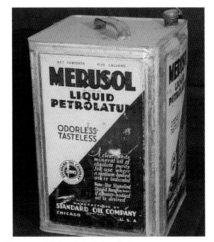

Merusol Liquid Petrolatum
five-gallon square tin can, Standard Oil, good condition.
$20+

Miquon Motor Oil
Standard Oil of California, two-gallon round tin can, excellent condition.
$20+

Miquon Motor Oil
Standard Oil of California, five-gallon square tin can, display side good condition, reverse fair.
$20+

Miss Pennsylvania Motor Oil
two-gallon tin can, fair condition.
$50+

Mobiloil Aero Gold Band
excellent condition, full.
$150+

Mobiloil Aero Red Band
tin quart, fair condition, some staining on top.
$40+

Three Mobil Anti-freeze
tin quarts, fair to good condition.
$40+ all

Mobiloil Filpruf
oil bottle, good condition, missing cap.
$125+

Mobiloil Gargoyle "A"
tin quart, fair to good condition, dents and wear.
$80+

Mobiloil Gargoyle "BB"
tin quart, foreign, fair condition, staining, small dents, full.
$70+

Mobiloil Gargoyle "BB"
foreign tin can, fair to good condition.
$70+

Mobiloil Gargoyle
one quart, excellent condition-plus.
$75+

Mobiloil Gargoyle "AF" Motor Oil
square one-gallon tin can, good condition.
$75+

Mobiloil Arctic Motor Oil
square one-gallon tin can, good condition.
$130+

Mobiloil Gargoyle Marine Motor Oil
square one-gallon tin can, fair condition.
$100+

Mobiloil Gargoyle 1940 Close-Out
three-gallon motor oil tin can, fair condition.
$150+

Mobil Delvac Oil 900 Series
tin quart, very good condition, some rust.
$60+

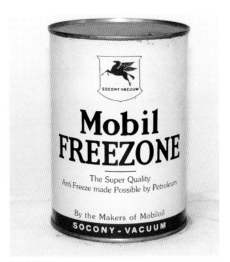

Mobil Freezone
tin quart, excellent condition.

$90+

Mobiloil and Mobiloil Outboard
tin quarts, both good condition.

$30+ pair

Mobiloil Outboard
tin quart, very good condition, dents.

$60+

Mohawk Chieftain Motor Oil
quart tin can, near mint, small scratch.

$400+

Monogram Motor Lubricants
five-gallon square tin can, excellent condition.

$90+

Monogram Motor Oil
quart tin can, single scratch.

$100+

Mother Penn
and Sterling Motor Oil tin quarts, excellent and
fair to good condition, respectively.

$130+ pair

Motoreze Motor Oil
and Union 76 anti-freeze (full) tin quarts, fair and
poor condition, respectively.

$30+ pair

Motorine and Filmoil
quart tin cans, excellent condition.

$30+ pair

Motor Life
motor oil quart tin can, near mint.
$35+

Motul H.D. Motor Oil
quart tin can, near mint.
$70+

Nanouk AntiFreeze
and Lo-Icy Lubricant quart tin cans, excellent condition.
$65+ pair

Navy Motor Oil
1/2-gallon tin can, good condition, no spout.
$120+

Northland and Gulf Gulfpride
quart tin cans, very good condition.
$15+ pair

Northland
and Barco Motor Oil, and Texaco anti-freeze tin quarts, all fair condition.
$60+ all

Two North Star
and one PS Motor Oil tin quarts, good condition.
$60+ all

Nourse Motor Oil
(green) quart tin can, excellent condition, light wear.
$175+

Nourse Motor Oil
(orange) quart tin can, excellent condition, small dent in front.
$175+

Nourse Motor Oil
five-quart tin can, good condition, full.

$75+

Oneida Motor Oil
quart tin can, near mint.

$190+

Opaline Motor Oil
(Sinclair) tin can, display side excellent condition,
reverse good.

$2,100+

Opaline Motor Oil
(Sinclair, striped) one-gallon tin, good condition.

$300+

Oronite Cleaning Fluid
one-gallon tin can, Standard Oil, fair condition.

$15+

Oronite Fly Spray
one-gallon tin can, Standard Oil, fair condition,
small dent.

$30+

Oronite Spring Oil
one-quart rectangular can, near mint.

$70+

Oronite Handy Oiler
with blue background, fair to good condition.

$40+

Oronite Lighter Fluid
oval 3 1/2-ounce tin can, excellent condition.

$110+

Oronite Lighter Fluid
dispenser with can insert, excellent condition, 16"
tall.

$900+

Two Oronite Handy Oilers
one with partial paper label, both very good
condition.

$300+ pair

Oronite Cleaning Fluid Free Sample
tin can, very good condition.

$80+

Oronite
shipping crate and one Oronite Spring Oil can.

$100+ pair

Pan-Am
1/2-gallon motor oil tin can, poor condition, wear
and dents.

$100+

Oronite Spring Oil
round pint tin can with spout, and Cleaning Fluid
1/4 pint can, both good condition.

$120+ pair

Para Pride Motor Oil
quart tin can, near mint.

$150+

Para Pride Motor Oil
tin quart, very good condition, small dent, wear.

$125+

Pearl Oil Kerosene
five-gallon square tin can, display side very good
condition, reverse fair.

$25+

Pennant 4D-Oil
for Fords 1/2-gallon tin can, light wear.

$160+

Penn Drake
motor oil quart jar, and Wm. Penn motor oil quart jar, very good and excellent condition.

$50+ pair

Penn Franklin
and Krieger Penn quart tin cans, both fair to good
condition.

$150+ pair

Penntroleum Motor Oil
quart tin can, excellent condition.

$200+

Pennzoil
with airplane and owls quart tin can, near mint.

$100+

Pennzoil
with owls quart tin can, near mint.

$80+

PEP Boys Pure as Gold Motor Oil
quart tin can, excellent condition, small dents.

$150+

Penn Empire
and Cycol Motor Oil five-gallon rocker cans, poor
condition.

$150+ pair

Phillips 66 Aviation
and Hancock one-quart oil cans (Hancock has
dents).

$60+pair

Phillips Trop-Artic
quart tin can, excellent condition, small dents.

$375+

Polarine
oil bottle, embossed Standard Oil Co., good
condition.

$50+

Polarine
embossed green one-quart oil bottle.

$350+

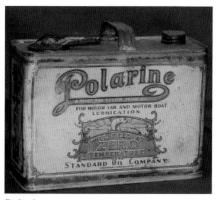

Polarine
with Polar Bear 1/2-gallon flat tin can, Standard
Oil Co., fair to good condition, wear and small
dents.

$90+

Polarine Motor Oil Heavy
double circle logo, half-gallon flat tin can, yellow
background, good condition with wear in field.

$225+

Polarine Motor Oil
1/2-gallon flat tin can, rectangular logo, yellow
background, good condition.

$300+

Polarine Motor Oil Medium
1/2-gallon flat tin can, excellent condition.

$140+

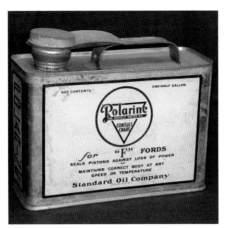

Polarine Motor Oil F
for Fords, 1/2-gallon flat tin can, excellent condition.

$130+

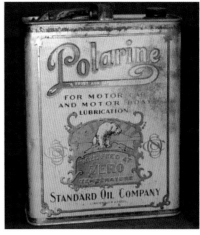

Polarine
with Polar Bear one-gallon flat tin can, Standard Oil Co., very good condition.

$60+

Polarine
one-gallon flat tin can, for lubrication of internal combustion motors, white on light green, good condition with normal wear.

$475+

Polarine
one-gallon flat tin can, for summer and winter, yellow background, fair condition, wear and some fading.

$100+

Polarine
five-gallon square tin can, large scenic, fair to good condition, wear and staining.

$400+

Polarine
five-gallon square tin can, small scenic, good condition, small dent on reverse.

$375+

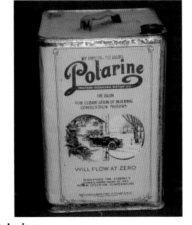

Polarine
five-gallon square tin can, double circle logo, "Will Flow at Zero," good condition, wear and minor dents.

$425+

Polarine
five-gallon square tin can, double circle logo, "Will Flow at Zero," green border, fair condition, wear and minor dents.

$200+

Polarine
five-gallon square tin can, double circle logo, "Heavy Grade," green border, fair condition, wear and minor dents.

$175+

Polarine/Standard
bottle with spout, good condition.

$40+

Polarine Motor Oil
five-gallon square tin can, atypical blue and red design, very good condition.

$25+

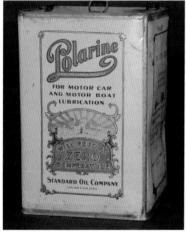

Polarine Motor Car & Boat Lubricant
five-gallon square tin can, Standard Oil, ship and mountains logo, very good condition.

$125+

Polarine Cup Grease
Standard Oil of New Jersey, five-pound round tin can, excellent condition.

$100+

Polarine Cup Grease
25-pound round tin can, Standard Oil (Ohio), excellent condition, dent in seam.

$25+

Polarine Fiber Grease
10-pound square tin can, with original wooden crate, very good condition.

$70+ set

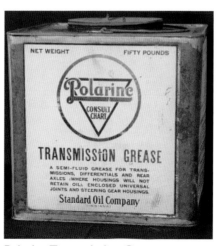

Polarine Transmission Grease
50-pound square tin can, excellent condition.

$70+

Polarine Transmission Grease "BB"
25-pound square tin can, car on reverse, very good condition.

$30+

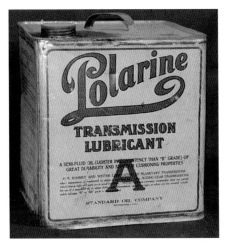

Polarine Transmission Lubricant "A"
25-pound square tin can, with green-label SoCo logo, very good condition.

$30+

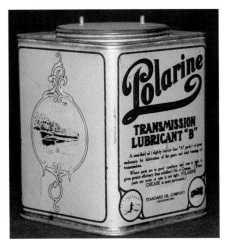

Polarine Transmission Lubricant "B"
five-pound tin can, green background, excellent condition.

$500+

Polarine Transmission Lubricant "B"
five-pound square tin can, very good condition.

$40+

Polly Penn Motor Oil
quart tin can, green stripe at top, excellent condition, light wear and dent on top.

$875+

Polly Prem Motor Oil
quart tin can, near mint, light wear.

$1,300+

Power-lube Motor Oil
five-gallon rocker can, display side excellent condition, reverse side fair.

$2,100+

Primrose
Waverly and Multipower Motor Oil tin quarts, all good condition.

$120+ all

Pure Tiolene
Linco Marathon, Mobil and Socony tall oil bottles.

$225+ all

Purity Oil Acme
transmission grease five-pound can.

$540+

Quaker Maid
and Quaker-Matic quart tin cans, both excellent condition.

$75+ pair

Racing Sta Lube
Premium and Regular quart tin cans, good to excellent condition.

$90+ pair

Real Penn Motor Oil
one-quart oil can, full, display side good condition, reverse poor.

$50+

Red Giant Motor Oil
quart tin can, very good condition, light wear.

$90+

Red Indian Ethylene Glycol Anti-Freeze
Imperial gallon can, fair to good condition.

$300+

Republic Motor Oil
tin quart, very good condition, small dents and some wear.

$150+

Richfield Handy Oiler
excellent condition.

$40+

Richfield Outboard Motor Oil
E-Z Mix tin quart, excellent condition.

$125+

Richfield Premium Motor Oil
tin quart, very good condition, some fading.

$50+

Richfield Premium Motor Oil
and Richlube Extra Duty Motor Oil tin quarts, very good condition.

$90+ pair

Richlube Premium Motor Oil
and Richfield Automatic Transmission Fluid tin quarts, both good condition.

$40+ pair

Richfield Super Anti-Freeze
quart tin can, excellent condition.

$30+

Richlube
Extra Duty and Richfield Circle C quart tin cans, excellent condition.

$70+ pair

Richlube HD
and Richfield Pennsylvania Motor Oil tin quarts, both excellent condition.

$50+ pair

Richlube Heavy Duty
and Motor Oil tin quarts, very good and fair condition, respectively.

$50+ pair

Richlube Super HD
quart tin can, near mint.

$45+

Richlube
Motor Oil and Richfield Circle C tin quarts, good and excellent, respectively.

$70+ pair

Richlube Motor Oil
(with early race car) one-gallon tin can, fair condition, wear and dents.

$600+

Richlube Motor Oil
five-quart tin can, excellent condition, no top.

$100+

Richlube HD
(round), Sinclair Pennsylvania Mobiline and BP Thermixine five-gallon rocker cans, poor condition.

$175+ all

Rich-Penn HD Motor Oil
tin quart, excellent condition-plus.

$140+

ROCO
Anti-Freeze and Richfield Motor Oil tin quarts, both good condition, small dents and wear.

$120+ pair

Royal Triton
three different tin quarts, fair to good condition, two full cans.

$100+ all

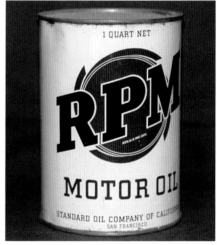

RPM Motor Oil
quart tin can, excellent condition, full.

$60+

RPM Aviation Oil
quart can, very good condition, has dents.

$75+

RPM Supreme Motor Oil
quart can, excellent condition.

$25+

RPM
three Sub-Zero, Special and Compounded tin quarts, all fair condition.

$40+ all

RPM
three Sub-Zero, Supreme and Special tin quarts, all fair to good condition.

$70+ all

RPM
two one-pound chassis grease cans, Heavy and HD, excellent condition.

$75+ pair

RPM
five different quart cans, fair to excellent condition.

$100+ all

RPM
Sub-Zero and Thermo-Charged Motor Oil tin quarts, both excellent condition.

$90+ pair

RPM
Thermo-Charged and S.O. Penn Motor Oil tin quarts, both good condition, some wear and dents.

$30+ pair

Sea Gull Motor
quart tin can, near mint.

$210+

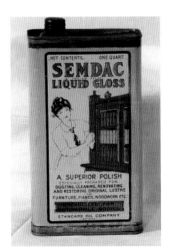

Semdac Liquid Gloss
Standard of Indiana, quart flat tin can, excellent condition.

$100+

Semdac Liquid Gloss
Standard of Indiana, one-gallon flat tin can, very good condition.

$125+

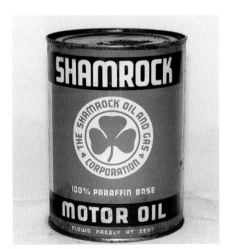

Shamrock Motor Oil
tin quart, very good condition, some wear, small dents, full.

$150+

Shell
25-pound Cup Grease tin can, fair condition.

$30+

Shell Aeroshell
tin quart, excellent condition, full.

$175+

Shell of California Motor Oil
flat one-gallon embossed tin can, display side good condition, reverse very poor.

$100+

Shell Outboard Motor Oil
two different tin quarts, both good condition, wear and fading.

$20+ pair

Shell
two sizes of tall embossed oil bottles.

$250+ pair

Shell Motor Oil
tall one-gallon tin can, early design, very poor condition, major dents in back.

$70+

Shell Golden Auto Oil
tall embossed one-gallon tin can, early design, very poor condition, wear and dents.

$150+

Shell Hand Separator Oil
embossed tall tin can, early design, fair condition.

$50+

Shell Motor Oil
embossed one-gallon tin can, early design, good condition.

$100+

Shell
tall oil bottle, good condition.

$80+

Shell Triple Motor Oil
British Imperial gallon tin can, fair condition.

$50+

Signal 4 Star
and Signal Premium Motor Oil tin quarts, excellent and poor condition, respectively.

$175+ pair

Signal Gasoline
two-gallon tin can with AC Spark Plug ad, fair condition.

$160+

Signal Penn Motor Oil
quart tin can, fair to good condition, light wear and significant dents.

$175+

Signal RPM DELO
tin can and Signal Motor Oil fiber can, fair to good and excellent condition, respectively.

$60+ pair

Signal RPM DELO
fiber and Signal HD tin quarts, good and poor condition, respectively.

$50+ pair

Signal Lubricants
one-pound grease can, very good condition.

$110+

Signal
one-gallon tin can, fair condition.

$90+

Silverol Motor Oil
tin quart, excellent condition, full.

$125+

Sinclair
Marine HD and Outboard Special (with screw lid) tin quarts, both very good condition.

$80+ pair

Sinclair
Marine HD and Extra Duty Outboard tin quarts, excellent condition.

$60+ pair

Sinclair Opaline
(white) full and Opaline (red) tin quarts, excellent and fair condition, respectively.

$90+ pair

Sinclair Opaline Motor Oil
one-gallon tin can, wear and small dents.

$140+

Sinclair Pennsylvania Motor Oil
(black dinosaur) tin quart can, fair to good condition, wear, no top.

$200+

Sinclair Turbo-S Oil
1048 Improved tin quart, good condition, small dents, wear, full.

$40+

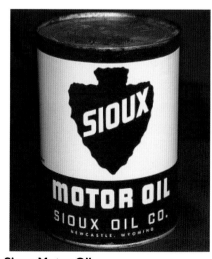

Sioux Motor Oil
quart tin can, excellent condition.

$100+

Sky Ranger Aviation Oil
quart tin can, excellent condition, small dents.
$225+

Skyway Motor Oil
quart tin can, very good condition, paint loss around top.
$175+

Skyway Motor Oil
tin quart with airplane, very good condition, some paint loss around top, full.
$400+

Socony Aircraft Oil
No. 2 five-gallon square tin can in original wooden crate, fair to good condition on three sides, back very poor.
$200+

Socony
one-gallon flat kerosene oil tin can, good condition, some edge wear.
$100+

Socony Motor Oil
embossed bottle, good condition.
$60+

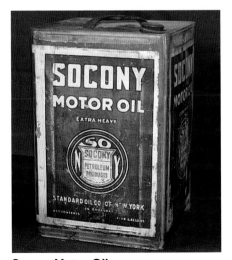

Socony Motor Oil
five-gallon square tin can, fair to good condition.
$20+

Socony Chassis Lubricant
one-pound grease can, fair to good condition.
$70+

Socony Cup Grease
five-pound square tin can, very good condition.
$25+

Socony Cup Grease
and Arctic Cup Grease, five-pound round tin cans, fair condition, staining and wear.

$30+ pair

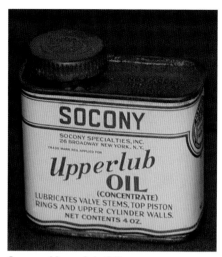

Socony Upperlub Oil
four-ounce can, excellent condition.

$80+

Socony General Petroleum Motor Oil
one-gallon tin can, display side fair to good condition, reverse poor.

$600+

Standard Oil Boston Coach Axle Oil
pint and Standard Hoof Oil, round pint, fair to good condition.

$25+ pair

Standard Oil Boston Coach Axle Oil
round pint and flat pint, very good condition.

$60+ pair

Standard Carriage Axle Oil
pint flat can, with cap spout, display side fair to good condition, reverse very poor.

$15+

Standard Oil Capital Cylinder Oil
one-gallon square tin can, front good condition, reverse fair, worn with small dents.

$275+

Standard Oil of Indiana
bottle with flame, good condition.

$70+

Standard Finol
and Gulf oval handy oilers.

$35+ pair

Standard Oil Fly Spray
pint and quart tin cans, both excellent condition.

$20+ pair

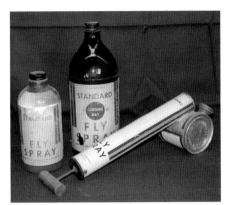

Standard Oil Fly Spray
pint and quart, and sprayer.

$35+ all

Standard Oil Co. Gas Engine Oil
one-gallon tin can, good condition.

$225+

Standard Hand Separator Oil
one-gallon square tin can, white background, fair
to good condition, small dents.

$90+

Standard Hand Separator Oil
(Indiana) one-gallon flat tin can, display side fair
to good, reverse poor to fair, wear and small dents.

$90+

Standard Hand Separator Oil
half-gallon rectangular short can, very good
condition.

$150+

Standard Hand Separator Oil
half-gallon rectangular tall can, fair condition,
dents.

$40+

Standard Household Lubricant
one-gallon square tin can, very good condition,
small dents.

$225+

Standard Oil of Indiana
and Atlanta Refining embossed one-quart oil
bottles.

$250+ pair

Standard Penn
quart tin can, very good condition.

$50+

Standard Oil Mica Axle Grease
25-pound grease bucket, fair to good condition,
light surface rust.

$40+

Standard Oil
two one-pound grease cans, excellent condition.

$100+ pair

Standard Shingle and Floor Oil
five-gallon square tin can, very good condition,
with original cardboard box (top missing).

$30+ set

Standard Oil Co. Hand Separator Oil
1/2-gallon square tin can, yellow background, very
good condition.

$225+

Standard Oil Stanavo
one-pound round grease can, fair condition, paper
label with tear.

$200+

Standard Stations Inc.
embossed oil bottle, with plastic spout, RPM
decal.

$80+

Standard Stations Inc.
embossed oil bottle, with plastic spout, RPM
decal.

$80+

Standard Stations Inc.
bottle with RPM Aviation decal.

$60+

Standard Stations Inc.
copper swing-spout one-gallon oil can, with embossed "Property of Standard Stations Inc.," good condition, wear and small dents.

$125+

Standard Transmission Lubricant
five-pound square tin can, fair to good condition, fading.

$40+

Strata Motor Oil
quart tin can, near mint.

$400+

Superol
(with rocket) and Aero (with plane) tin quarts, excellent and poor to fair condition, respectively.

$50+ pair

Superol
and PENNtroleum quart tin cans, excellent condition.

$25+ pair

Texaco 574 Oil
quart tin can, excellent condition.

$60+

Texaco Marine Motor Oil
tin quart, good condition, minor dents and wear, full.

$80+

Texaco Motex
and Insulated Motor Oil tin quarts, both good condition, both full.

$40+ pair

Texaco Motor Oil
and New Motor Oil tin quarts, both good condition, some wear.

$40+ pair

Texaco StarJet-5 Turbine Oil
tin quart, excellent condition, no top.

$30+

Texaco Outboard Motor Oil
three different tin quarts, all good condition.

$40+ all

Texaco Spica Oil
pint can, excellent condition.

$100+

Texaco Marfak
five-pound tin can, good condition, has wear.

$60+

Texaco Thuban Compound
five-pound tin can, excellent condition.

$175+

Texaco Motor Oil
one-gallon square tin can, fair to good condition, wear and soiling.

$100+

Texaco
one-gallon motorcycle oil tin can, good condition.

$180+

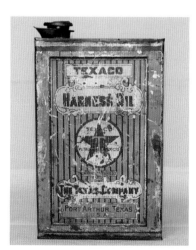

Texaco Harness Oil
one-gallon tin can, poor to fair condition, wear and small dents.

$45+

Texaco
1/2-gallon motor oil tin can, excellent condition.
$325+

Texaco
"squatty" one-gallon motor oil tin can, good condition.
$675+

Texaco Valor Motor Oil
two-gallon tin can, very good condition.
$60+

Texaco
1/2-gallon motor oil tin can, very good condition.
$175+

Texaco
(Port Arthur) three grease and oil cans, poor to fair condition.
$80+ all

Texaco
four outboard motor oil cans and two Texaco outboard motor oil bottles, fair condition.
$80+ all

Texaco
three Port Arthur oil cans, good condition or less.
$75+ all

Texaco
five aircraft oil cans.
$120+ all

Texaco
rustproof compound, water pump grease, roof cement and motor cup grease cans.
$60+ all

Texaco Marfak
Texwax and radiator cleaner compound containers.

$100+ all

Texaco
two oil bottles, and one embossed Havoline oil bottle.

$275+ all

Thermo Anti-Freeze
quart tin can, small dents and a stain on side.

$30+

TP Aero Motor Oil
five-quart tin can, fair to good condition.

$525+

Triton
and Royal Triton Motor Oil tin quarts, good and excellent condition, respectively.

$60+ pair

Trojan
and Tidewater quart tin cans, excellent condition.

$40+ all

Tydol
and Veedol Motor Oil quart tin cans, both excellent condition.

$125+ pair

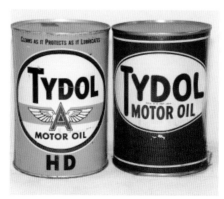

Tydol Flying A
and Tydol Motor Oil tin quarts, good condition, some wear, small dents.

$100+ pair

Union Valve Lubricant Oil
one-gallon tin can, good condition.

$90+

Union 76 Triton Motor Oil
quart tin can, excellent condition, small dent.

$30+

Valvoline Motor Oil
one-gallon tin can (early design), display side
excellent condition, reverse fair to good.

$150+

Vanderbilt Motor Oil
quart tin can, near mint, small dent in bottom
ring.

$400+

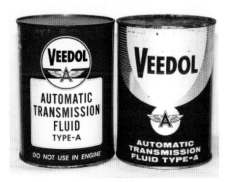

Veedol Automatic Transmission Oil
two different tin quarts, both good condition,
small dents and wear.

$160+ pair

Veedol HD+
and Veedol Economy Motor Oil tin quarts, both
excellent, small dents.

$120+ pair

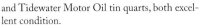

Veedol
and Tidewater Motor Oil tin quarts, both excellent condition.

$60+ pair

Veedol Motor Oil
three different tin quarts, two very good condition,
one fair, dented.

$70+ all

Veltex Household Oil
can, excellent condition, light wear and scratches.

$425+

Veltex Motor Oil
one-gallon tin can, very poor condition.

$70+

Veltex Lubricant
one-pound grease can, good condition, no lid.
$110+

Veltex Penn Motor Oil
quart tin can, near mint.
$575+

Vico "U" Motor Oil
one-gallon tin can, display good condition, reverse fair.
$300+

Waverly WOW
and Troco quart tin cans, near mint condition and fair to good, respectively.
$110+ pair

White Rose Motor Oil
Imperial quart tin can, near mint.
$50+

Whiz Metal Polish
cone top, half pint can, excellent condition.
$225+

Whiz Roadside Hand Cleanser
12-ounce flat tin can.
$250+

Wil-Flo Motor Oil
quart tin can, near mint, extra fine.
$475+

Wil-Flo Motor Oil
tin quart, near mint, full.

$350+

Zenoil 2000 Mile Motor Oil
tin quart, poor to fair condition, dents, wear.

$60+

Zerolene Motor Oil
one-quart tin, excellent condition, some wear around base.

$275+

Zerolene Medium
1/2-gallon flat tin can, with Polar Bear, poor to fair condition, dull finish.

$25+

Zerolene No. 3
1/2-gallon flat tin can, with round bear logo, fair condition, dent in back, cap with logo.

$25+

Zerolene No. 6
1/2-gallon flat tin can, with round bear logo, very good condition, cap with logo.

$140+

Zerolene Zero Cold Test
1/2-gallon tin can, with motor boat, car and SOCO logo on reverse, fair to good condition.

$225+

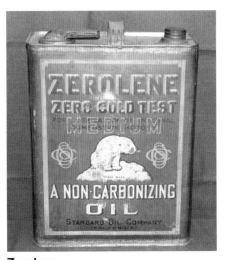

Zerolene
with polar bear and Model T on back, one-gallon square tin can, fair to good condition, some wear and dents.

$250+

Zerolene
with polar bear and Model T on back, one-gallon square tin can, poor condition, some surface rust, wear and dents.

$25+

Zerolene for Motor Cars No. 3
one-gallon square tin can, very good condition, small dents.

$300+

Zerolene for Motor Cars No. 5
one-gallon square tin can, very good condition.

$225+

Zerolene Gear Grease
five-pound square tin can, display side fair, reverse poor, wear and dents.

$25+

Zerolene Gear Oil
one-gallon square tin can, excellent condition.

$70+

Zerolene
one-gallon tin can, with bear, and Model T on side, fair to good condition, small dent on side.

$125+

Zerolene Heavy
with bear five-gallon square tin can, blue background, with motor boat and touring car, fair to good condition.

$175+

Zerolene for Motor Cars No. 5
five-gallon square tin can, good condition, with embossed pump.

$125+

Zerolene Cup Grease
50-pound square tin can, wire handle, good condition.

$75+

Zerolene Cup Grease
five-pound tin can, good condition.

$25+

Zerolene Motor Oil No. 7
with bear logo, five-gallon square tin can, fair condition, wear and small dents.

$25+

Zerolene High Pressure Lubricant
five-pound round tin can, tall version with cloud logo, good condition.

$10+

Zerolene Cup Grease
five-pound round tin can, short version with cloud logo, good condition.

$25+

Zerolene Gear Lubricant
five-gallon round bucket, display side fair to good, reverse poor.

$25+

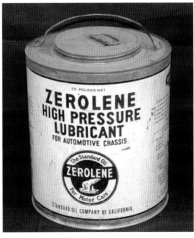

Zerolene High Pressure Lubricant
25-pound round tin can, display side good condition, reverse fair, small dents.

$90+

Zerolene Cup Grease
five-pound tin can, very good condition.

$25+

Zerolene Cup Grease
(blue background) 25-pound round tin can, display side good condition, reverse fair, also has SoCo logo.

$15+

Zerolene Cup Grease
one-pound grease can, fair to good condition.

$50+ all

Zerolene Transmission Lubricant "A"
25-pound square tin can, fair condition, wear and dents.

$10+

Zerolene Transmission Lubricant "BBB"
50-pound square tin can, display side excellent condition, reverse good.

$100+

Zerolene Transmission Lubricant "A"
five-pound square tin can, very good condition.

$30+

Zerolene Valve Oil
one-quart rectangular can with glass dispenser, can fair condition on display side, poor to fair on reverse.

$10+ pair

Zerolene Valve Oil
one-quart rectangular can, display side very good condition, reverse fair to good, dents.

$40+

Zerolube Winter Motor Oil
quart oil can, good condition.

$70+

Zerolene
1/2-gallon motor oil tin can, poor to fair condition.

$80+

Zerolene
1/2-gallon non-carbonizing oil tin can, very poor condition, has fading and wear.

$45+

Zerolene Medium Motor Oil
one-gallon tin can, good condition, faded.

$125+

Zerolene No. 5 Motor Oil For Cars
one-gallon tin can, fair condition.

$50+

Zerolene Wheel Bearing Grease
five-pound can, good condition.

$50+

Zerolene Type "F" Motor Oil
five-gallon square tin can, good condition.

$100+

Zerolene Gear Grease
50-pound tin can, excellent condition, some small dents.

$250+

Displays, Holders, Racks

Although this category may be of limited interest to many collectors, those trying to assemble a well-rounded collection that approximates a working garage find them to be the perfect accessories for display. This section also includes rack tops, which many collectors use as wall-mounted decorations.

Calso
map rack, good condition, paint loss at bottom, 20" by 13".

$175+

Chevron Credit Card
application rack, very good condition, minor paint loss, 8" by 4".

$100+

Chevron Supreme Gasoline
map rack, excellent condition, 20" by 13".

$300+

Chevron
Men and Women restroom key holders, plastic and metal, good condition, worn.

$100+ pair

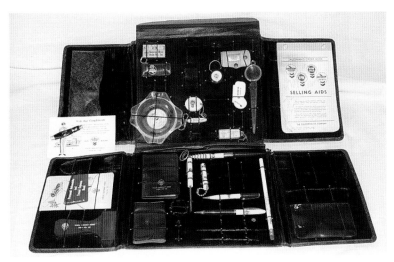

Chevron Sales
sampler kit in vinyl case, good condition.

$300+

Cities Services
oil rack, 37" tall, repainted.

$225+

Gulf
oil can rack, tin sign.

$130+

KEYS *to our* clean REST ROOMS

MEN   LADIES

PLEASE RETURN KEYS TO HOOKS

GULF

Gulf
restroom tin key holder, dated 1961, excellent condition, 9" by 11".

$210+

Mobiloil
six-bottle metal holder, with bottles and spouts.

$750+ all

Gulf Oil
counter-top display, with original cans, near mint.

$1,200

ISO-VIS
quart can metal rack.

$425+

Mobiloil
six-bottle rack with lift-out center and six generic bottles and spouts.

$525+ all

Mobil Gargoyle
oil can rack top, double-sided tin, fair to good condition, 11" by 24".

$125+

Mobiloil Marine
oil can rack top, double-sided tin, very good condition, 11" by 24".

$625+

Mobiloil Gargoyle
oil cabinet, restored, with globe holder, 88" by 28" by 28", with two Mobiloil Gargoyle single-sided porcelain signs, both excellent condition.

$1,500+

Mobiloil Special Double-Sided Tin
sign for oil rack, excellent condition, 11" by 21".

$250+

Mobil Tires
display rack with ad insert, 8 1/2" by 14".

$325+

Oronite Products
metal display rack, light wear, wood base, 19" by 14 1/2" by 12".

$125+

Phillips 66
The World's Finest Oil double-sided porcelain oil rack top, near mint, 12" by 20".

$1,300+

Polarine
oil viscosity display, 14" by 12", good condition, some staining.

$175+

Polarine Motor Oil
viscosity tin display rack, fair condition, faded, 10" by 10".

$25+

RPM Motor Oil
20-gallon drums on roll-about rack, 47" by 42", overall.

$250+

RPM
10-bottle oil rack with decals, near mint.

$200+

RPM 10-30 Special Motor Oil
double-sided tin rack top, near mint, 9" by 16".

$125+

RPM Motor Oil First Choice
single-sided tin rack top, excellent condition, flange on bottom edge, 8" by 22".

$400+

RPM
12-bottle metal rack in original condition, with bottles and spouts, 19" by 29".

$700+ all

RPM Motor Oil Thermo-Charged
oil rack, with 12 bottles and spouts, 18" by 28", base has been powder coated, original decal worn.

$700+ all

RPM
round metal oil can rack, holds 18 cans, with three cans (very good condition).

$350+

Shell
automatic burner oil, Olympic Diesel Fuel Supply Co. sample display with bottle.

$300+

Shell
metal 12-bottle oil rack with 12 generic bottles and spouts, fair to good condition.

$375+ all

Shell
metal 12-bottle oil rack with 11 generic bottles and spouts, fair to good condition.

$525+ all

Shell
restroom key holder single-sided tin with fiber-glass keys, dated 1967, near mint, 8 1/2" by 12".

$225+

Shell Service
tin map rack, early design, poor condition, 11" by 9".

$150+

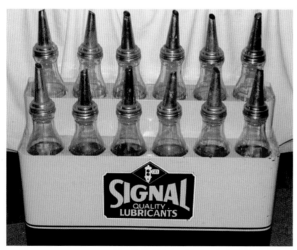

Shell X-100 Motor Oil
display rack.

$550+

Signal
metal 12-bottle oil rack with 12 generic bottle and spouts, fair to good condition.

$575+ all

Sinclair HC Truesdell Oil Co.
reorder box, new in box.

$100+

Six-oil bottle metal rack
full of Standard Penn bottles, all with spouts, rack
repainted, 26" by 16" by 11".

$250+ all

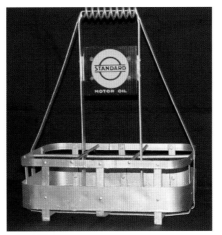

Six-oil bottle metal rack
with two Standard Oil of New Jersey single-sided
porcelain signs, rack repainted.

$275+

Socony Petroleum Products
tin counter top display rack, light wear, 13" by 17"
by 8".

$175+

Socony Petroleum Products
single-sided tin die-cut display rack, good condition, chip in field, 14" by 16".

$300+

Standard Heating Oils
sample display, excellent condition, 6" by 11".

$50+

Standard Heating Oils
sample display, excellent condition, 8" by 8".

$50+

Standard ISO-VIS D
motion paper display, good condition, 3 1/2" by 8".

$50+

Standard Oil of New Jersey Products
tin rack, fair condition, includes pint and half-pint
cans, 17" by 12" by 6".

$100+ all

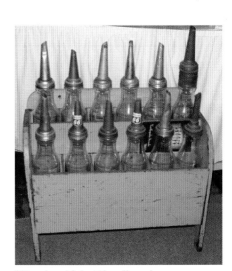

Wooden 12-bottle oil rack
with bottles and spouts.

$250+ all

Globes

The globes that once decorated the tops of gasoline pumps are the holy grail for many petroliana collectors.

Early globes were a single piece of glass, often with etched or painted lettering. "Globe" is a misnomer, since none here is truly spherical, and a complete globe often has three main parts: two lenses and a body, though some came with a single lens.

The body can be made of metal, plastic or fiberglass. A high-profile body has a standing seam around the circumference. A low-profile body has a flattened seam. A gill body has a rubber or metal gasket holding the lenses in place. Later Capco bodies are molded plastic with screw fasteners at the base. A hull body accepts notched lenses, and is open where the lenses are mounted, as opposed to a glass body where the lenses rest on a low dome. Gill and hull bodies take their names from the manufacturers that created them, but as the petroliana field has grown, these names are often found with lower-case spellings.

Some collectors secure the lenses on the bodies using silicone caulk, a practice that many object to because this can contribute to paint loss and it makes the lenses difficult to examine off the bodies.

Ripple and jewel bodies are among the most desirable, and hardest to find. Ripple glass bodies have an irregular textured surface, and come clear, white, and in a range of colors. Jewel bodies have round faceted glass "jewels" set into the surface.

Globes can range in value from $50 for a common or damaged example to almost $20,000 for rarities in near-mint condition.

At the end of this section we have included listings for fantasy and reproduction globes and lenses.

American Gas globe
15" lenses in low-profile body, display side good condition, reverse fair.

$400+

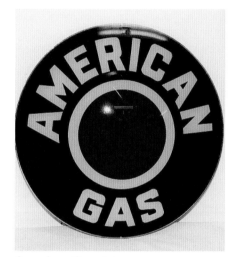

American Gas globe
13 1/2" single lens, no body, very good condition.

$50+

American Hi-Compression globe
13 1/2" lenses in a gill-glass body, small chip on one lens.

$1,800+

Aro Flight globe
13 1/2" lenses in a gill body, excellent condition.

$1,400+

Ascot Gasoline globe
with boat-tail racecar, 15" lenses in high-profile body, very good condition, very rare.

$17,000+

Associated Gasoline
"More Miles to the Gallon" globe, 15" lenses in high-profile metal globe, minor paint flaking around edge of one lens, reverse has small spot of paint loss, body repainted.

$1,800+

Associated White Gold globe
15" single lens in low-profile body, excellent condition.

$1,200+

Atlantic globe
13 1/2" lenses on gill body, excellent condition.

$375+

Atlantic Hi-Arc globe
13 1/2" lenses in a gill body, very good condition.

$450+

Atlantic Gasoline
one-piece chimney-top globe, etched lettering, slight fading, chimney repainted, small chips on base.

$5,250+

Atlantic Imperial globe
13 1/2" lenses in a gill body, excellent condition.

$425+

Atlantic Imperial globe
13 1/2" lenses in a gill body, lenses excellent, body has chip to base.

$450+

Atlantic Premium globe
13 1/2" lenses on a gill glass body, excellent condition.

$400+

Bay globe
13 1/2" lenses in Capco body, good condition.

$175+

Bay Bronze globe
13 1/2" lenses in original Capco body, good condition.

$300+

Beacon Gasoline globe
13 1/2" lenses in gill glass body, light scratches to field, ring and base repainted.

$3,000+

Bell globe
with derrick, 13 1/2" single lens in a white ripple body, lens very good condition, body with cracked base.

$900+

Bell Ethyl globe
13 1/2" lenses on a gill body, excellent condition.

$1,550+

Bell Regular globe
13 1/2" lenses, in a wide white glass body.

$800+

Bell Regular globe
13 1/2" lenses in a white ripple body, display side good condition, minor fading and scratches on reverse.

$1,800+

Ben Franklin Premium-Regular globe
13 1/2" lenses in a red ripple body with copper base.

$7,500+

Blue Crown
one-piece, possibly original paint, 17" tall, metal collar. (Collector Tip: The blue Crown is the rarest color, followed by gold and red.)

$800+

Boron D-X globe
13 1/2" lenses, in a wide white glass body.

$500+

Browder Regular 76 Gasoline globe
13 1/2" lenses in Capco body, good condition.
$300+

Buffalo Premium
single 13 1/2" lens, excellent condition.
$275+

Bull's Head Products globe
16 1/2" lenses in high-profile metal body, both lenses have been professionally restored (less than 15 percent).
$1,700+

Calpet
single 15" lens, fair condition, overall thin paint.
$150+

Calso Gasoline globe
15" lenses on high-profile fiberglass body, excellent to near mint, minor scratches.
$350+

Calso Gasoline globe
13 1/2" lenses on gill body, lenses excellent condition, body has base crack.
$400+

Calso's Supreme Gasoline globe
with Ethyl logo, 15" single lens in a high-profile metal body, near mint.
$1,600+

Carter globe
13 1/2" lenses in Capco body, excellent condition.
$250+

Carter Extra globe
13 1/2" lenses in Capco body, lenses very good condition, body broken.
$225+

Chevron Gasoline globe
15" lenses in a high-profile metal body, excellent condition, minor scratches.

$1,700+

Chevron Gasoline globe
13 1/2" lenses on a high-profile metal body, both lenses poor condition with paint loss.

$675+

Chevron Supreme Gasoline globe
15" lenses in a high-profile fiberglass body, near mint.

$2,300+

Chevron Supreme globe
15" lenses in low-profile body, very good condition.

$925+

Cities Service globe
clover-shaped lenses (caulked in), very good condition.

$2,200+

Cities Service Koolmotor globe
14" lenses in a wide clover-shaped glass body, very good condition.

$3,200+

Citizens "77" globe
15" lenses in high-profile metal body, some fading, back of lenses over-sprayed, body repainted.

$600+

Citizens Ethyl globe
15" single lens in low-profile metal body, light scratches in field.

$750+

Clark globe
13 1/2" lenses, in a wide white glass body.

$300+

Cliff Brice
oval lenses in oval glass body, excellent condition.
$800+

Clipper
(airplane) oval lenses in Capco body, very good condition.
$2,700+

Coastal Gasoline
(with birds) globe, 13 1/2" lenses in a clear ripple body.
$2,750+

Conoco globe
with Ethyl logo, 13 1/2" lenses, green plastic body.
$900+

Conoco Gasoline
(with Minuteman) globe, 15" lenses in a high-profile metal body (repainted).
$5,750+

Conoco globe
15" lenses in high-profile body, lenses very good condition.
$650+

Conoco globe
13 1/2" lenses in Capco body, lenses very good condition, body has small chip.
$225+

One Conoco globe
13 1/2" lenses, no body, very good condition.
$225+

Co-op globe
(red, Superior, Wis.), 13 1/2" lenses, in a gill body, with copper collar.
$350+

Co-op Gasoline globe
single lens in a narrow glass body, excellent condition.

$2,000+

Crescent Gasoline globe
15" lenses in a high-profile metal body, very good condition.

$3,200+

Crown Gasoline
(Kentucky) globe, 16 1/2" lenses, good condition, paint loss at edges of lenses.

$700+

Crown Gold globe
13 1/2" lenses in a gill body, with metal base, excellent condition.

$575+

Crown Silver globe
13 1/2" lenses in a gill body, with metal base, excellent condition.

$550+

Deep Rock globe
13 1/2" lenses, wide white glass body, reverse has 2" crack.

$350-$550

Derby Gasoline globe
13 1/2" lenses, gill body.

$500+

Dieso-Shell
one-piece glass clam.

$350+

Dieso-Shell
(foreign) one-piece glass clam, letters repainted, chip in base.

$250+

Dixie globe
13 1/2" single lens in Capco body, good condition.
$225+

Dixie Power to Pass globe
13 1/2" lenses in a gill glass body, very good condition.
$1,200+

Drake's Hi Octane Regular globe
13 1/2" lenses in a Capco body, excellent condition.
$3,200+

DX Marine Gasoline
single lens, good condition.
$350+

Eagle Gasoline globe
13 1/2" lenses on a yellow ripple gill body, excellent condition.
$3,750+

Elreco Regular globe
13 1/2" lenses in a gill body, with metal base, very good condition.
$900+

Ethyl globe
13 1/2" lenses, in a wide white glass body.
$1,000+

Fleet-Wing globe
13 1/2" lenses in narrow glass body with metal base, excellent condition.
$2,200+

Fleet-Wing Golden globe
13 1/2" lenses in a narrow glass body, excellent condition.
$800+

Flight Gasoline globe
15" lenses on high-profile fiberglass body, one lens has green arrow, one has blue-green arrow.
$1,450+

Flight Gasoline
(Chevron) globe, 15" lenses in high-profile fiberglass body, very good condition.
$2,000+

Flying A Associated globe
15" lenses in low-profile body, display side good condition with paint thinness and spotting, reverse poor, cracked, paint loss.
$900+

Flying A globe
13 1/2" lenses, in a narrow white glass body.
$800+

Flying A Kerosene globe
13 1/2" lenses in gill body, excellent condition.
$3,000+

Flying A Kerosene lens
cracked in two.
$100+

Flying A Super Extra
"shoe box" one-piece glass, excellent condition.
$500+

Frontier Rarin'-To-Go globe
13 1/2" lenses, in a wide white glass body.
$1,400+

Frontier Rarin'-To-Go globe
13 1/2" lenses in a Capco body, good condition.
$1,200+

Fuel Oil globe
13 1/2" lenses in Capco body, excellent condition.
$75+

Fyre-Drop globe
15" lenses in high-profile metal body, display side very good condition, reverse has small spider-web crack in "E."
$1,500+

Fyre-Drop globe
15" lenses in fiberglass high-profile body, display side very good, reverse fair with paint loss.
$2,000+

Fyre-Drop globe
13 1/2" lenses, in a high-profile metal body, near mint.
$2,200+

Fyre-Drop globe
(early design), 15" lenses with paint flaking in center of field, high-profile metal body.
$1,000+

Gasolene one-piece globe
with etched glass, old repaint, chips around base.
$475+

Gasoline globe
one-piece white glass, old repaint, etched, circa 1920, 15 1/2" diameter, base chips.
$500+

General Gasoline globe
15" single lens in repainted low-profile body, excellent condition.
$600+

General Petroleum Ethyl globe
15" single lens on a low-profile body, good condition.

$2,100+

General Petroleum Ethyl globe
13 1/2" lenses on narrow glass body, display side excellent condition, reverse very good with small chip.

$1,600+

Gilmore Blu-Green globe
15" lenses in repainted high-profile body, excellent condition.

$10,250+

Gilmore Ethyl globe
15" single lens in low-profile body, good condition.

$3,500+

Gilmore Red Lion
plus Tetraethyl globe, 15" lenses in repainted high-profile body, excellent condition, heavily caulked in place.

$18,500+

Gilmore Roar with... globe
15" lenses in repainted high-profile body, lenses in good condition with light staining.

$7,000+

Globe
(with map) globe, 13 1/2" lenses in a gill body with metal base, light scratches.

$1,600+

Gold Crown
one-piece, possibly original paint, worn, 17" tall, metal collar.

$600+

Golden Flash globe
13 1/2" lenses in a narrow glass body, lenses have slight fading around edges, body very good.

$500+

Go Mileage Mart globe
13 1/2" lenses in wide glass body, good condition, lenses caulked.

$3,750+

Green Streak globe
15" lenses in high-profile body, display side excellent condition, reverse very good.

$2,750+

Guaranteed Measure globe
15" punched tin lenses, all original, worn paint.

$750-$1,250

Gulf Marine White globe
12 1/2" lenses in glass body, display side very good condition, reverse good, has chip and crack at base.

$1,800+

Gurney Seed globe
13 1/2" lenses, showing radio station, Yankton, S.D., in a wide white glass body.

$1,500+

Hercules Ethyl Gasoline globe
13 1/2" lenses, in a wide white glass body.

$1,800+

A selection of Gulf globes in Rich Gannon's collection, including a rare one-piece, etched Gulf Kerosene example, $2,500+. Other values, from left: $700, $500, $1,800 and $1,600.

Hiotane globe
13 1/2" lenses in Capco body, minor fading.
$1,300+

Hi-Power
(Heccolene) globe, 15" lenses in high-profile body, lenses very good condition with light scratches.
$1,400+

Hi-Power Ethyl
(Heccolene) globe, 15" low-profile body, lenses excellent condition, body good, original paint.
$2,100+

Hudson globe
13" lenses in red ripple body.
$3,750+

Hudson Ethyl
with logo, 13" lenses in an orange ripple gill body, body cracked with paint loss around base.
$3,250+

Hudson Ethyl globe
13 1/2" single lens, Capco body.
$1,000-$1,500

Hudson Regular globe
13 1/2" lenses, Capco body.
$2,000-$2,500

Husky globe
13 1/2" lenses, white glass gill body, base chips.
$2,800+

Husky Hi-Power
(with dog) globe, 13 1/2" lenses on a Capco body.
$3,750+

Imperial
(Canada) three-star globe, 16 1/2" lenses, texture-painted metal body.

$550-$750

Imperial No Lead globe
13 1/2" lenses, new Capco body.

$200-$350

Imperial Norcolene Oil and Gasoline globe
15" lenses near mint condition, high-profile body in original paint, only one known.

No established value

Imperial Refineries Ethyl globe
near mint, 13 1/2" lenses, in a wide white glass body.

$800+

Imperial Refineries Ethyl globe
13 1/2" lenses, wide white glass body with base chips, reverse has one edge chip.

$450-$650

Indian Gas globe
13 1/2" lenses in hull glass body with metal base ring, dated 1936, good condition.

$1,300+

Indian Gas globe
13 1/2" lenses in screw-base hull body, very good condition.

$1,000+

Johnson Gasolene Time Tells
(with ethyl logo) globe, 13 1/2" lenses in orange ripple gill body, metal base.

$5,750+

Jumbo Gas
(elephant) globe, 13 1/2" lenses, in a banded glass body, back has light scratches in field.

$900+

Kan-O-Tex Bondified globe
13 1/2" lenses, in an orange ripple glass body, base chips.

$3,000+

Kan-O-Tex
star and sunflower globe, 13 1/2" lenses, in a red ripple glass body.

$2,000+

Kan-O-Tex
star and sunflower globe, 13 1/2" lenses in a white ripple body, light scratches.

$1,600+

Kan-O-Tex with Ethyl
13 1/2" lenses, in a wide white glass body.

$1,800+

Kendall Polly Power globe
single 13 1/2" lens, with bullet impact spot lower right, gill glass body.

$250-$350

Knight Kerosene globe
13 1/2" lenses in a Capco body, display side very good, reverse lens cracked.

$1,300+

Liberty Gasoline globe
15" lenses in low-profile metal body.

$2,750+

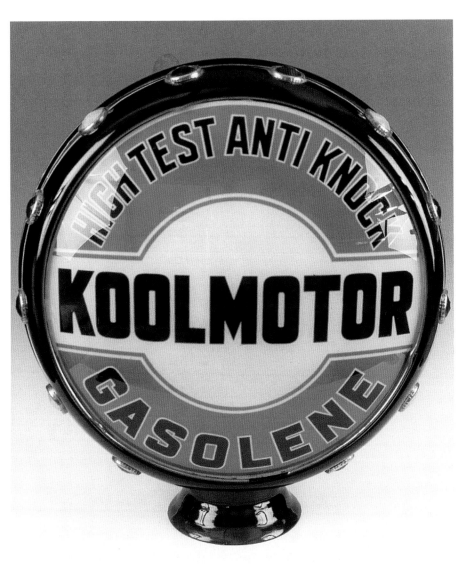

Koolmotor
jewel-body globe, 15" lenses, 19 1/2" tall overall, circa 1930s, excellent condition.

$5,000+

Lion globe
13 1/2" lenses in a wide glass body, reverse has scratches.

$950+

Lion Knix Knox globe
13 1/2" lenses in narrow glass body, copper base.

$2,500+

Lonas Premium globe
13 1/2" single lens in original red Capco body with some crazing, lens good condition, scratches in field.

$100+

Magnolia Gasoline globe
16 1/2" lenses in high-profile metal body, lenses very good condition, body repainted.

$2,750+

Magnolia globe
with rose, 16 1/2" lenses in low-profile body, very
good condition.

$4,600+

Marathon globe
15" lenses in a high-profile metal body, display
side excellent condition, small scratches on reverse.

$2,100+

Marathon Mile Maker globe
with runner, 13 1/2" lenses in a new glass body,
excellent condition, lenses probably new old stock.

$800+

Marathon Mile-maker globe
13 1/2" lenses, in a wide white glass body.

$1,000+

Marine Oil-Blended Gasoline globe
13 1/2" single lens in wide glass body, lens
cracked, body chipped.

$225+

McQuerter Red Hat Gasoline globe
15" lenses in a high-profile metal body, lenses
professionally restored (less than 15 percent), body
repainted.

$950+

Metro globe
15" single lens in repainted low-profile body, lens
good condition with paint loss, chipping.

$275+

Metro globe
15" lenses in repainted low-profile body, very good
condition.

$275+

Metro globe
13 1/2" lenses, narrow white glass body, reverse
lens has minor paint wear.

$350-$550

Metro
15" single lens with Sun-Kerosene General Petroleum Corp. sticker, good condition.

$200+

Metro
15" lenses, no body, both good condition.

$225+ pair

Midland globe
13 1/2" lenses, in a white plastic body.

$200+

Midland Co-op globe
15" lenses, late 1920s.

$3,000+

Midland Wholesale globe
13 1/2" lenses in a white glass gill body.

$2,500+

Minnesota Farm Bureau Gasoline globe
13 1/2" lenses, in a gill body.

$4,000+

Minuteman
lenses, 10 1/2" and 12", no body, both excellent condition.

$50+ pair

Mobil
(foreign) one piece glass square, has hairline crack and small hole.

$175+

Mobilfuel Diesel globe
13 1/2" lenses in Capco body, excellent condition.

$250+

Mobilfuel Diesel globe
15" single lens in repainted low-profile body, lens good condition, light staining at bottom.

$550+

Mobiloil Gargoyle
large oval globe, one-piece body, excellent condition, probably new old stock.

$2,900+

Mobilgas Aircraft globe
15" single lens in low-profile body, lens broken.

$300+

Mobilgas Ethyl globe
15" lenses in high-profile body, display side very good condition, reverse excellent.

$450+

Mobilgas Ethyl globe
15" lenses in high-profile body, excellent condition.

$575+

Mobilgas Ethyl globe
15" single lens in high-profile body, very good condition.

$400+

Mobilgas
one-piece 36B pump topper in good condition.

$700+

Mobilgas globe
13 1/2" lenses on glass body, excellent condition.
$350+

Mobilgas globe
13 1/2" lenses in Capco body, fair condition.
$175+

Mobilgas globe
16 1/2" lenses in high-profile body, very good condition.
$550+

Mobilgas globe
(rare green letters), 15" lenses in repainted low-profile body, very good condition.
$600+

Mobilgas Marine globe
16 1/2" single lens in low-profile body, lens good condition, minor fading.
$550+

Mobilgas Special globe
13 1/2" lenses, in a wide white glass body.
$600+

Mobilgas Special globe
(made in England) one-piece glass baked body, cracked.
$275+

Mobilgas Special globe
15" lenses in high-profile fiberglass body, display side very good condition, reverse good.
$375+

Mobilheat Stove Oil globe
13 1/2" lenses in red hull body with hairline, display side very good condition, reverse good with slight paint loss.
$1,050+

Mobil Kerosene globe
15" lenses in high-profile body, lenses very good condition, reverse has minor paint loss at edge.
$2,000+

Mobil Premium globe
13 1/2" lenses in Capco body, excellent condition.
$250+

Mobil Regular globe
13 1/2" lenses in Capco body, excellent condition.
$200+

Mohawk Gasoline
(orange background) globe, 15" lenses in low-profile metal body (repainted).
$8,500+

Mutual Gasoline globe
15" lenses in low-profile metal body, light scratches.
$1,700+

Mutual Gasoline globe
(Ethyl), 15" lenses in low-profile metal body, light scratches.
$700+

National Benzole Mixture
(foreign), one-piece glass, display side fair condition, reverse poor, badly faded.
$350+

North Star globe
13 1/2" lenses in glass body, excellent condition.
$800+

Oil Creek Ethyl globe
with logo, 15" lenses in high-profile metal body,
light scratches, minor fading on reverse, body
repainted.

$4,800+

Oriole Gas globe
15" lenses in high-profile metal body, reverse has
scratches.

$4,500+

Penn-Drake Blue Blood globe
13 1/2" lenses in a gill body, display side good
condition with light scratches on one side, reverse
excellent.

$3,750+

Penreco globe
15" lenses in high-profile metal body, lenses
professionally restored (less than 15 percent), only
one known.

$1,750+

Pepco Gas Independent globe
15" lenses in high-profile metal body, both lenses
professionally restored (less than 14 percent).

$500+

Phillips 66 Flite-Fuel
plastic shield globe, both sides have light scratches.

$500+

Phillips 66 globe
13 1/2" lenses, in a wide white glass body.

$900+

Phillips Unique globe
13 1/2" lenses, in a wide white glass body.

$2,500+

Pioneer globe
15" lenses, high-profile metal body.

$500+

Plymouth automobile globe
16 1/2" lenses in high-profile metal body, very
good condition.

$2,100+

Premier globe
with Ethyl logo, 13 1/2" lenses, in a narrow white
glass body.

$600+

Products of the Pure Oil Co. globe
13 1/2" lenses, in a wide white glass body.

$850+

Pump top
with four Chevron ad glasses in good condition.

$450+

Pure Purol-Pep globe
13 1/2" lenses in a wide glass body, very good
condition.

$750+

Pure Purol-Pep globe
15" lenses, in a high-profile metal body.

$800+

Purol Ethyl globe
15" lenses, in a high-profile metal body.

$900+

Pyramid
15" lenses, no body, one very good condition, one
good with minor edge chips.

$250+ pair

Ranger Gasoline
(with eagle) globe, in while gill body.

$1,300+

Red Crown
one-piece glass, repainted.
$250+

Red Crown
one-piece globe, old repaint, 17" tall, metal collar.
$350+

Red Crown globe
15" lenses in repainted high-profile body, fair condition, display side has thin paint, reverse touched up.
$1,400+

Red Crown Ethyl globe
has 2" hole in lower section, fair to good condition.
$250+

Red Crown Gasoline globe
15" lenses on high-profile metal body, 7" base, display lens good condition with fading, reverse fair with fading and minor paint loss.
$1,000+

Red Crown Gasoline globe
with crown, 15" lenses in high-profile metal body, display side excellent, reverse very good.
$3,750+

Red Crown Gasoline
(California) globe, 15" lenses in a high-profile metal body, near mint.
$1,700+

Red Crown Gasoline
(Indiana) globe, 16 1/2" lenses in a high-profile metal body, display lens very good condition with minor staining, reverse fair with fading.
$500+

Red Feather globe
13 1/2" single lens in a Capco body, excellent condition.
$1,200+

Red Indian globe
13 1/2" lenses in narrow body globe with copper base, good condition.

$2,750+

Regal Oil Refining globe
15" single lens, in high-profile metal body (re-painted).

$2,750+

Richfield (bulls-eye) globe
15" lenses in high-profile fiberglass body, excellent condition.

$1,000+

Richfield Hi-Octane globe
15" lenses in high-profile metal body, lenses excellent, body repainted.

$900+

Ride with Rose Regular Gasoline globe
13 1/2" single lens in Capco body, very good condition.

$2,750+

Rock Island globe
13 1/2" lenses in narrow body globe with copper base, good condition.

$2,100+

Save-More System Ethyl globe
13 1/2" lenses, wide white glass body, new old stock.

$750-$1,250

Save-More System Regular globe
13 1/2" lenses, wide white glass body, new old stock.

$750-$1,250

Shamrock globe
13 1/2" single lens, Capco body (damaged).

$100-$150

Shamrock oval globe
body damaged, lenses very good condition.
$200+

Shell clam
white glass, etched, old possibly original paint, 17 1/2" tall.
$800+

Shell
one-piece etched glass body, display side good condition, reverse fair.
$425+

Shell Diesoline
(foreign) one-piece glass clam, excellent condition.
$325+

Shell globe
(East Coast), 15" single lens in high-profile body, lens fair condition with two small touchups on shell, paint loss on outer ring, body repainted.
$700+

Shell
(English) one-piece glass clam, body and paint excellent condition.
$275+

Shell globe
(West Coast), 15" single lens in high-profile body, lenses very good condition, body good original paint.
$2,500+

Shell
(Silver) one-piece glass clam, 2" by 3" hole in side.
$125+

Shell
(Super) one-piece glass clam, original paint on both sides good condition, large chips out of base (not visible when mounted on pump).
$700+

Shell
(Super) Ethyl one-piece glass clam, body and paint excellent condition, probably new old stock.
$1,350+

Shell
(Super) Ethyl one-piece glass clam, body and paint very good condition.
$1,200+

Shell
(Super, foreign) one-piece glass clam, body excellent condition, letters repainted.
$350+

Signal globe
15" lenses in high-profile body, lenses excellent condition, body repainted.
$10,000+

Signal
(with light) globe, 15" lenses in high-profile metal body, light scratches to field, body repainted.
$5,500+

Silver Comet globe
with black eagle, 13 1/2" lens on narrow glass body, good condition.
$1,150+

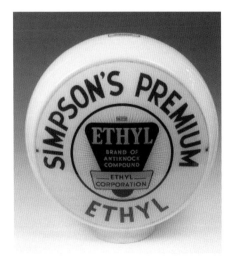

Simpson's Premium Ethyl globe
13 1/2" lenses, in a wide white glass body.
$750+

Sinclair Aircraft
one-piece globe, baked-on paint faded with some pinholes, chips around base.
$6,000+

Sinclair Diesel globe
13 1/2" lenses in narrow glass body, lenses excellent condition, body unacceptable.
$350+

Sinclair Dino Supreme globe
13 1/2" lenses in Capco body, excellent condition.
$175+

Sinclair Ethyl globe
13 1/2" lenses in a narrow glass body, excellent condition, lenses possibly new old stock.
$850+

Sinclair H-C globe
13 1/2" lenses in wide glass body, very good condition.
$500+

Sinclair H-C globe
13 1/2" lenses in Capco body, lenses excellent condition, body good.
$150+

Sinclair H-C globe
(old dark green) 13 1/2" lenses in a narrow glass hull body, very good condition.
$500+

Sinclair Marine globe
13 1/2" lenses in Capco body, excellent condition.
$600+

Sinclair Oils
one-piece globe, etched, 15" tall.
$2,000+

Sinclair Pennant
13 1/2" lenses in very good condition.
$1,000+ pair

Skelly Gasoline
(three stars) globe, 13 1/2" lenses, in a wide white glass body.

$400+

Skelly globe
13 1/2" lenses, in a wide white glass body.

$250+

Skelly Aromax globe
with Ethyl logo, 13 1/2" lenses, in a wide white glass body.

$400+

Skelly Fortified Gasoline globe
(two stars), 13 1/2" lenses, in a wide white glass body.

$450+

Skelly Fortified Premium globe
(two stars), 13 1/2" lenses, white plastic body.

$500+

Skelly Keotane globe
(four stars), 13 1/2" lenses, in a wide white glass body.

$200+

Skelly Powermax globe
13 1/2" lenses, white glass body.

$300+

Skelly Premium globe
13 1/2" lenses, in a narrow white glass body.

$400+

Skelly Premium globe
(three stars), 13 1/2" lenses, in a wide white glass body.

$400+

Skelly Regular globe
(three stars), 13 1/2" lenses, in a wide white glass body.

$400+

Skelly Regular globe
(three stars), 13 1/2" lenses, white plastic body. (Collector Tip: Skelly globes with an "S" that appears to have a raised profile are older than the globes with a flat "S.")

$300+

Smith-O-Lene Aviation Gasoline globe
12 1/2" lenses on wide glass body, reverse lens cracked.

$3,750+

Smith-O-Lene Ethyl globe
12 1/2" lenses in glass body, very good condition.

$7,000+

Sohio Marine Gasoline globe
13 1/2" lenses on wide glass body, excellent condition.

$1,600+

Solite Gasoline globe
15" lenses, high-profile metal body.

$1,000+

Sovereign globe
13 1/2" lenses, in a gill body.

$600+

Speedway globe
13 1/2" lenses in a narrow glass body, excellent condition.

$4,000+

Spur Gas Gasoline globe
13 1/2" single lens in red ripple body, excellent condition.

$4,200+

Super Major globe
with Ethyl logo, 13 1/2" lenses, in a narrow white
glass body.

$500+

Standard "Bar and Circle" globe
15" lenses on low-profile metal body, lenses good
condition with fading.

$600+

Standard Gasoline
(Chevron) globe, 15" lenses in low-profile body,
good condition, body in old repaint.

$950+

Standard Kerosene globe
15" single lens in repainted high-profile body, lens
excellent condition.

$600+

Standard Red Flame
one-piece glass, paint is faded.

$250+

Standard Red Flame
one-piece glass, very good condition, minor paint
loss to base.

$450+

Standard Red Flame
one-piece glass, in excellent condition, original
paint, probably new old stock, screw base.

$550+

Standard Gasoline
(California) globe, 15" lenses in a high-profile
metal body, near mint.

$1,200+

Standard Marine globe
13 1/2" lenses in glass body, very good condition.

$550+

Standard Oil Ethyl Gasoline globe
15" lenses in a low-profile metal body, early Ethyl logo, excellent condition, minor staining.
$1,300+

Standard Oil Flight Gasoline globe
15" lenses in a high-profile fiberglass body, near mint.
$750+

Standard's Supreme
(with Ethyl) Gasoline globe, 15" lenses in a high-profile metal body, excellent to near mint, minor scratches.
$2,300+

Sunoco
(Blue) globe, 15" lenses, fiberglass body, very good condition.
$550+

Sunray Ethyl globe
13 1/2" lenses in original red Capco body, possibly new old stock.
$1,900+

Sunray Gasoline globe
13 1/2" lenses in a Capco body, very good condition, small chips at mounting holes.
$1,750+

Super Greyhound Motor Fuel globe
13 1/2" lenses on a narrow-body with metal base, very good condition, minor chips around edge on display side lens.
$6,500+

Texaco
(white T) globe, 13 1/2" lenses, in a narrow white glass body.
$600+

Texaco
embossed one-piece glass globe, mint condition, probably new old stock, with copper screw base.
$1,900+

Texaco globe
one-piece glass body, very good condition.

$1,600+

Texaco
(black T) globe, 13 1/2" lenses in narrow glass body, display side excellent condition, reverse good with staining.

$550+

Texaco Diesel Chief globe
13 1/2" lenses in Capco body, display side excellent condition, reverse good with light paper marks.

$750+

Texaco Ethyl
(black T) globe, 15" lenses, in a high-profile metal body.

$2,000+

Texaco
leaded stained-glass metal body globe, slight fading, smaller size.

$4,500+

Texaco Sky Chief
(black T) globe, 13 1/2" lenses, in a narrow white glass body, with copper collar, flaking to edges.

$550+

Texaco Sky Chief
(white T) globe, 13 1/2" lenses in narrow glass body, excellent condition.

$700+

Texaco Sky Chief
(black T) globe, 13 1/2" lenses, dated 1939, in hull body, with crimped metal base, good condition.

$650+

Texas Rose Regular globe
13 1/2" lenses in Capco body, excellent condition.

$2,000+

Thrifty Gas globe
with Scottie logo, 13 1/2" lenses, in a wide white glass body.

$1,800+

Tower Gasoline
(with tower) globe, 13 1/2" lenses in a wide glass body, reverse has 1/2" flaw on edge.

$2,900+

Trophy globe
13 1/2" lenses, gill body, Minneapolis origin.

$1,400+

Trophy globe
13 1/2" lenses in a gill body with metal base, good condition, scratches in field.

$1,600+

Tydol Ethyl globe
16 1/2" lenses, repainted low-profile metal body.

$850-$1,250

Tydol Ethyl globe
16 1/2" lenses, in a high-profile metal body.

$1,000+

Tydol globe
16 1/2" lenses in repainted low-profile body, very good condition.

$500+

Tydol globe
with Flying A, 13 1/2" lenses, significant wear to front, reverse cracked, in a wide white glass body.

$300+

Union 76 globe
15" single lens in high-profile body, very good condition.

$700+

Union 76 Gasoline globe
15" single lens in low-profile body, very good
condition.

$1,600+

Union 76 + Tetraethyl globe
15" single lens in high-profile body, good condition, chip at bottom of lens.

$2,300+

Union Ethyl globe
15" single lens in low profile body, lens in very
good condition, small flake at 2 o'clock and small
chip at 3 o'clock.

$1,300+

Union Non-Detonating Gasoline globe
15" single lens in new high-profile body, lens very
good condition.

$2,400+

Union White Magic globe
15" lenses in low-profile body, display side very
good condition, reverse good.

$900+

Union White Magic globe
with car decal over Unoco, 15" single lens in low-
profile repainted body, lens in very good condition.

$1,000+

United Ethyl globe
13 1/2" lenses, Capco body, minor edge chip on
one lens.

$200-$350

United Gasoline Hi-Test globe
13 1/2" lenses, minor edge flaking, Capco body.

$350-$550

Unoco (Union) globe
15" single lens in high-profile body, very good
condition.

$275+

Utility Gasoline
(with map) globe, 13 1/2" lenses in a gill body, excellent condition.

$1,800+

Valvoline Go-Mix Outboard Fuel globe
13 1/2" lenses in Capco body, excellent condition.

$700+

Veltex globe
15" lenses in high-profile body, display side excellent condition, reverse good, body in good original paint.

$1,300+

Viking globe
13 1/2" lenses in a Capco body, display side excellent condition, reverse very good with scratches in field.

$2,000+

Visible Measure
one-piece etched globe, letters repainted, small chips around base.

$300+

VS
(Volunteer State) globe, 13 1/2" lenses in original green Capco body, excellent condition.

$250+

VS Ethyl
(Volunteer State) globe, 13 1/2" lenses in original green Capco body, excellent condition.

$300+

Wadhams Mobilgas globe
15" single lens in high-profile body, lens fair condition, staining and paint loss.

$900+

Wadhams Metro globe
13 1/2" lenses in wide glass body, display side good condition, reverse fair with minor paint loss and yellowing. (Collector Tip: Some petroliana enthusiasts refer to yellowing as "ambering.")

$550+

Wadhams True Gasoline
one-piece chimney-top globe, etched glass, slight fading.

$5,500+

Walburn Ethyl globe
15" lenses in a high-profile metal body, excellent condition.

$1,050+

Webb Cut Price Regular globe
13 1/2" lenses, new Capco body, display side near mint, reverse broken, Minnesota origin.

$350-$500

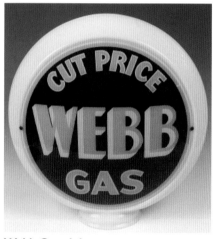

Webb Gas globe
13 1/2" lenses, in a narrow white glass body, from Waseca, Minn.

$800+

White Eagle
one-piece, pointed nose, full feathers, 20 1/2" tall, late 1920s. (Collector tip: The blunt-nose example of the eagle is the most common.)

$2,800+

Western Motor globe
(with cowboys), 13 1/2" lenses in a narrow glass body.

$8,000+

White Eagle
one-piece glass, has crack in neck.

$1,000+

White Eagle
one-piece, 21 1/4" tall, late 1920s, bullet impact. (If perfect, $2,300+.)

$900+

White Flyer globe
13 1/2" lenses in a banded glass body, very good condition.

$2,100+

White Rose National Ethyl globe
13 1/2" lenses, in a narrow white glass body.

$1,000+

White Rose globe
13 1/2" lenses on narrow glass body, lenses caulked in place.

$1,900+

White Rose Gasoline
(boy with chalkboard) globe, 15" single lens in re-painted high-profile body, lens in good condition with some paint loss around edge.

$2,200+

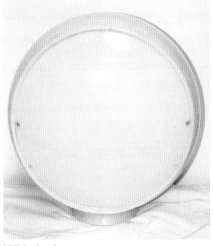

Wide body
glass globe.

$110+

Wood Hi-Test globe
13 1/2" lenses in wide glass body, lenses have been professionally restored (less than 15 percent).

$500+

Wood Oils Gasoline globe
13 1/2" lenses in wide glass body, lenses have been professionally restored (less than 15 percent).

$800+

New metal globe bodies
15" and 13 1/2".

$150+ pair

Old metal globe bodies
two 15".

$220+ pair

Associated Gasoline
reproduction single lens in Capco body.

$90+

Reproduction and Fantasy Globes

There is almost no area of antique collecting that is not plagued by fakes and reproductions. For collectors of vintage gas and oil items, the only way to avoid reproductions is experience: Mmaking mistakes and learning from them; talking with other collectors and dealers; finding reputable resources (including books and Web sites), and learning to invest wisely, buying the best examples one can afford.

Beginning collectors will soon learn that marks can be deceiving, paper labels and tags are often missing, and those that remain may be spurious. Adding to the confusion are "fantasy" pieces, globes that have no vintage counterpart, and that are often made more for visual impact than deception. Examples of these are included here.

How does one know whether a given piece is authentic? Does it look old, and to what degree can age be simulated? What is the difference between high-quality vintage advertising and modern mass-produced examples? Even experts are fooled when trying to assess qualities that have subtle distinctions.

There is another important factor to consider. A contemporary maker may create a "reproduction" sign or gas globe in tribute of the original, and sell it for what it is: a legitimate copy. Many of these are dated and signed by the artist or manufacturer, and these legitimate copies are highly collectible today. Such items are not intended to be frauds.

But a contemporary piece may pass through many hands between the time it leaves the maker and winds up in a collection. When profit is the only motive of a reseller, details about origin, ownership and age can become a slippery slope of guesses, attribution and—unfortunately—fabrication.

As the collector's eye sharpens, and the approach to inspecting and assessing petroliana improves, it will become easier to buy with confidence. And a knowledgeable collecting public should be the goal of all sellers, if for no other reason than the willingness to invest in quality.

Fortunately, there are entire Web pages devoted to petroliana reproductions. A check of these resources is advised for beginning collectors.

Buick Sales–Service
reproduction lenses in Capco body.

$75+

Chevrolet Corvette
reproduction single lens in Capco body.

$75+

Chevrolet Sales–Service
reproduction lenses in Capco body.

$100+

Conoco Minute Man
reproduction lenses in Capco body.

$62.50+

Dixie
reproduction globe, in Capco body.

$50+

Ford Sales–Service
reproduction lenses in Capco body.

$137.50+

General Petroleum Corp.
reproduction lenses in Capco body.

$190+

Gilmore Blu-Green
reproduction 13 1/2" single lens.

$105+

Gilmore Red Lion
+ Tetraethyl reproduction 15" lenses in high-profile body.

$450+

Grizzly
reproduction 15" lenses.

$120+ pair

Husky
reproduction globe, in Capco body.

$95+

Mobil Regular
reproduction lenses in Capco body.

$62.50+

Mohave Oil Co.
fantasy globe, made for Disney, in Capco body.

$225+

Mohawk Ethyl
reproduction 15" single lens in high-profile body
with original paint.

$150+

Mohawk Gasoline
reproduction 15" lenses in repainted high-profile
body.

$175+

Oldsmobile
reproduction lenses in Capco body.

$50+

Polly Gas
reproduction lenses in Capco body.

$50+

Pontiac Service
reproduction lenses in Capco body.

$50+

Red Crown
reproduction globe, in Capco body.

$50+

Richfield Hi-Octane
reproduction lenses in Capco body.
$75+

Seaco Aviation Fuels
reproduction lenses in Capco body.
$180+

Shell
reproduction lenses in Capco body.
$37.50+

Shell "Roxanne"
reproduction 15" lenses.

$150+ pair

Standard Aviation Products
fantasy globe, made for 20th anniversary "Gas Bash," 15" lenses on high-profile metal body.
$525+

Sunray Gasoline
reproduction lens in Capco body.
$105+

Union Gasoline
reproduction 13 1/2" lenses in metal body, body dented.
$62.50+

White Rose No-Knock
reproduction lenses in Capco body.
$75+

Pumps

Pumps are not for everybody. They are big machines that—though relatively simple—can require significant maintenance if a collector desires to keep them in working order. That's why most serve as nonfunctioning accessories. Correct components and spare parts can be expensive, and proper restoration in manufacturer's colors can take months. As you will see here, pumps in untouched original condition are quite rare, and command some of the highest prices.

Some sellers, easily found on the Internet, stock reproduction parts for many gas pumps. Some also offer new-old-stock parts, used parts, and original-condition and restored pumps. Others carry globes, decals, signs, books, oil cans, road maps, and offer restoration, consultation and appraisals.

This section also includes "lubsters," better known as oil pumps.

20-gallon lubster
professionally restored, with original Zerolene sign.

$225+

Bennett E450
double clock-face pump, restored in Shell colors and decals (peeling).

$3,250+

Bennett EM-150
clock-face pump, old repaint, no glass in front, with globe holder.

$1,700+

Bennett Model 748 pump
restored in Gulf colors, with reproduction globe.

$950+

Bennett 766 pump
painted in Sinclair colors, with reproduction globe.

$950+

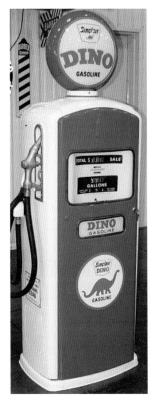

Bennett 996
computing pump restored in Sinclair colors, with reproduction Dino globe, side door missing glass.
$1,000+

Bennett
(?) computing pump restored in Sinclair colors, with reproduction H-C globe.
$1,300+

Bowser 318 Varley Sentry
round clock-face pump, old repaint, globe holder, no ad glass, back glass broken.
$1,700+

Bowser 80
(?) quarter-sawn oak cabinet, with leaded beveled window at bottom, top windows beveled (one missing), center pump for gasoline, side pumps for oil, refinished.
$5,000+

Bowser 410 Xacto Sentry
clock-face pump, restored in Signal colors, with reproduction Signal globe and decal.
$1,700+

Boyle-Dayton Model 174
10-gallon visible pump, original paint (crazed)
with Gilmore Blu-Green decals, cylinder cloudy.
$4,400+

Clear Vision 550
10-gallon visible pump, restored, with globe
holder, brass riser pipes, no lights.
$1,000+

Eaton Serv-Self
clock face coin-operated pump in original condition.
$3,250+

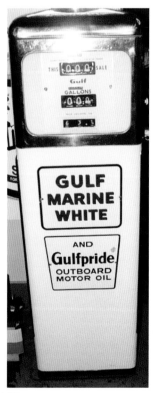

Erie 158
computing pump, made for Gulf, good condition,
with globe holder.
$400+

Erie Pump
1930 calendar page, framed, good condition, 32"
by 20".
$150+

Fry Guaranteed 117
ten-gallon visible pump, restored, with globe
holder and lights, cylinder etched "Fry."
$2,200+

Hayes 1923
10-gallon visible pump, with storage door, old repaint.

$1,100+

Hayes AX600C
2-in-1 Cash Recorder clock-face pump, no glass, needs restoration.

$1,900+

Hayes
(?) Wichita visible pump, may be cut down, repainted in Texaco colors, with reproduction Texaco globe (1982) in a Capco body.

$1,000+

M&S 80 Script Top
Conoco N-tane pump, restored, Conoco pump plate, no glass in back.

$1,500+

M&S 80 Script Top
Conoco Ethyl pump, restored, decals.

$1,300+

M&S 80 Script Top
Mobilgas Special pump, restored, face plated on reverse has chips.

$1,700+

M&S 80 Script Top

Mobilgas pump, restored, some wear, reverse script has crack in letter.

$1,200+

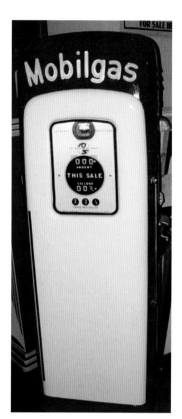

M&S 80 Script Top

Mobilgas computing pump, restored.

$1,500+

M&S 80 Script Top pump

Mobilgas Special, with reproduction pump plates.

$1,800+

National 10

computing pump, missing one ad glass, window cracked, has globe holder, good condition.

$1,800+

National A-38 pump

with Chevron Supreme gasoline glass, original paint, some rust.

$850+

National A-38

pump, with Chevron Supreme ad glasses and sticker, professionally restored.

$2,700+

National A-38 pump
with Flying A ad glass, no globe holder, no inside
face plate, overall good condition.

$900+

National 90
clock-face pump, Apex dials, old repaint, no glass,
sheet metal damaged above one dial.

$1,100+

National 90
(?) Apex clock-face pump, restored in Shell colors
and decal.

$1,100+

National 365
computing pump with 64 top, Flying A ad glass,
good original condition.

$850+

Rheem
porcelain clock-face pump, repainted in Sunoco
colors, good condition.

$1,300+

RPM
10-gallon lubster, original paint, very good condition.

$50+

Southwest Model 1 pump
with Gulf stickers.

$700+

Tokheim
Model ? 10-gallon visible pump restored in
Texaco colors, missing globe.

$2,750+

Tokheim 36-B pump
painted in Texaco colors, with reproduction globe,
two original Fire Chief porcelain pump plates
dated 1957 and 1962.

$1,700+

Tokheim 39
(?) double computing pump, restored, with
reproduction Mobilgas and Mobilgas Special
globes, original ad glasses in front, none in other
openings.

$3,200+

Tokheim 39-SL
Stationliter computing pump, display side with
good paint, reverse faded, Mobilgas Special ad
glass and pump plate.

$1,450+

Tokheim 285
(?) 10-gallon visible pump with hail screen, with
lights, old repaint needs restoration.

$1,000+

Tokheim 850
clock-face pump, professionally restored, with Red Crown sticker.

$2,750+

Tokheim 850
clock-face pump, fair repaint, with globe holder.

$1,500+

Tokheim Interceptor pump
good original condition.

$50+

Unknown visible pump
10-gallon, restored in Union colors.

$1,000+

Unknown oil dispenser
six-station, air-operated, fair condition.

$2,700+

Unknown visible gas pump
10-gallon, repainted in Flying A colors, with reproduction Flying A globe.

$950+

Wayne 40
computing pump, fancy face bezel, original paint fair condition, Mobil shield, globe holder.

$1,400+

Wayne 40
computing pump, fancy face bezel, old repaint, good condition, Mobilgas Special porcelain pump plate.

$1,000+

Wayne 40A
computing pump, no sight gauge, needs repaint, no glass in openings, has globe holder.

$700+

Wayne 50 Showcase
computing pump, restored, Mobilgas decals, all glass shelves and windows.

$4,250+

Wayne 50 Showcase
computing pump, original condition, no glass or shelves.

$4,250+

Wayne 60
computing pump, repainted pink, bottom made into shelves with latch.

$800+

Wayne 60 pump
with sunburst, restored in Gilmore colors, several parts chromed, with reproduction Gilmore globe, also fitted with remote button that makes dial register.

$3,500+

Wayne 60 pump
painted in Phillips 66 colors, with reproduction globe.

$2,250+

Wayne 60-S
computing showcase pump, Sinclair H-C ad glass, with shelves and windows, missing bottom metal panel.

$2,000+

Wayne 71
showcase computing pump, restored in Sinclair colors, Sinclair H-C ad glass and stickers, with globe holder, very good condition.

$3,000+

Wayne 80 pump
with Flying A Gasoline ad plate, repainted, with reproduction Flying A globe, no back, no works, converted to beverage dispenser.

$550+

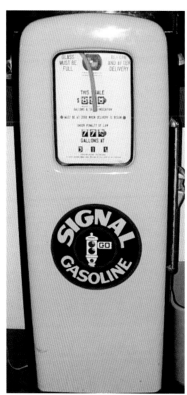

Wayne 80
computing pump, restored in Signal colors and decals.

$800+

Wayne 80
computing pump, restored in Signal colors and decals, with reproduction Signal globe.

$700+

Wayne 80
computing pump with Mobilgas Marine ad glass (none in back), bottom with original paint, Mobilgas Special porcelain pump plate.

$850+

Wayne 80
computing pump with Conoco Ethyl Script top, restored.

$1,300+

Wayne 80 Script Top
for Mobilgas pump, good condition, touched-up chips, cracks in lettering.

$650+

Wayne 80 Script Top
for Mobilgas pump, fair condition, touched-up chips, cracks in lettering.

$575+

Wayne 80 Script Top
for Sunoco Dynafuel pump, poor condition.

$575+

Wayne 452
twin 5-gallon cylinder visible gas pump, cylinder has etched gallon mark, with globe holder and lights, needs paint.

$4,000+

Wayne 491-F
Greek Column 10-gallon visible pump, air operated original paint and Mobilgas decals.

$9,000+

Wayne 491-F
Greek Column 10-gallon visible pump, air operated, original paint and Mobilgas Ethyl decals.

$8,000+

Wayne 492
Greek Column 10-gallon visible pump, hand operated, restored in Union colors.

$4,750+

Wayne 515F
10-gallon visible pump restored in Magnolia colors, with reproduction globe and curved pump plates.

$3,000+

Wayne 519
10-gallon visible pump restored in Shell colors and decal.

$1,200+

Wayne 519
(?) 10-gallon visible pump, no cylinder or top, may be missing more parts.

$275+

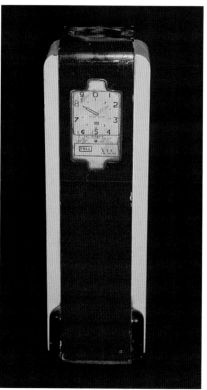

Wayne 866
clock-face pump, has Metro ad glass, needs paint, no globe holder.

$1,300+

Wooden display model
of Eaton Serv-Self coin-operated pump, good condition, some wear, 16 1/2" by 5 1/2".

$125+

Signs

Every collecting area has its own language that presents a challenge for beginners. Aumann Auctions Inc. of Nokomis, Ill., a dominant force in the selling of petroliana, uses a number system, primarily to describe the condition of signs and containers. This system ranges from 10 (new in the box) to 1 (a total loss), but most pieces generally fall into the range of 5 (bad) to 9.5 (near mint). These numbers are established by considering the condition of labels, paint and porcelain, scratches, dents, chipping, extra holes, normal and excessive wear, fading, bending and warping. Add to this the factors that determine desirability, like graphic impact, rarity and regional collecting tastes, and you can see how difficult it might be for a group of collectors to be unanimous in their assessment of a given piece of petroliana.

Because not all sellers use a similar numbering system, and since opinions about value can vary—sometimes widely—from collector to collector, we are using the following descriptions that are used by enthusiasts in almost all collecting areas: near mint, excellent, very good, good, fair to good, fair, poor to fair, poor, very poor and bad.

Ace High Motor Oil
late 1920s, single-sided tin, 20" by 13 1/2".

$2,500

Admiral Penn
single-sided tin, 20 1/2" by 10 1/2".

$1,000

Aladdin Security Oil
single-sided porcelain sign, Standard Oil New Jersey, with original paper label, near mint, edge chip, 12" square.

$1,700+

All Credit Cards Accepted
(Cliff Brice) double-sided porcelain sign, touched up chips around mounting holes, and large area in lower corner, 24" by 36".

$75+

Amalie Motor Oil
tin flange sign, dated 1948, display side excellent condition, reverse good with scratch, 15" by 22".

$400+

Amoco
(?) "Sanitary Rest Room Inspected" single-sided porcelain sign, very good condition, staining in field, 7" diameter.

$400+

Aristo Motor Oil
porcelain flange, very good condition, small chips in field, reverse has two quarter-size chips, 20" by 20".

$2,500+

Aristo Union Gasoline
"Speed & Power" double-sided porcelain sign, display side good-plus condition with quarter-size chip in field and around edges, reverse fair to good condition, 32" by 26".

$2,500+

Associated Lubrication
Factory Specified single-sided tin sign, bad condition, 22" by 158".

$200+

Associated Motor
Diesel Fuel double-sided porcelain sign, display side very good condition with small chips in field, reverse good, 48" diameter.

$1,000+

Atlantic
double-sided porcelain sign, fair condition, 9" by 13".

$60+

Atlantic Premium
porcelain pump plate, near mint, new old stock, 11" by 13".

$150+

Atlantic Refining Co.
porcelain pump plate (collectors call this shape the "scrambled egg"), excellent condition.

$875+

Atlantic White Flash
porcelain pump plate, excellent condition, dated 1950, 17" by 13".

$350+

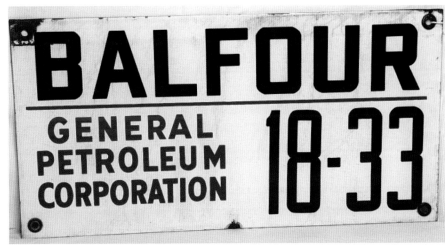

Balfour General Petroleum Corp.
18-33 double-sided porcelain sign, good condition, 12" by 24".

$80+

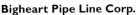

Bigheart Pipe Line Corp.
two caution signs, both excellent condition, larger 8" by 12".

$175+ pair

BP
double-sided porcelain die-cut shield, fair condition, 29" by 29".

$300+

Brown's-Oyl for Fords
(with Brownie) single-sided tin sign, near mint,
20" by 13".

$800+

Bulko Gasoline
porcelain pump plate, excellent condition, small
chip at right mounting hole, 11" by 12 1/2".

$3,500+

Cargray Gold
porcelain pump plate, near mint, new old stock,
10" diameter.

$400+

Calso Gasoline
porcelain pump plate, very good condition, one
scratch touched up.

$200+

Calso Gasoline
porcelain pump plate with hallmark, excellent
condition, 12" by 15".

$500+

Calso Gasoline
porcelain pump plate, near mint, 12" diameter.

$250+

Calso Gasoline
single-sided porcelain pump plate, excellent condition, 11" diameter.

$225+

Calso Gasoline
single-sided porcelain die-cut pump plate, excellent condition, small chips around edges, 14" by
11".

$375+

Calso Gasoline Unsurpassed
double-sided porcelain curb sign, good condition,
chips in field and around edge, original base, 30"
diameter without base.

$650+

Calso RPM Lubrication
porcelain flange, display side excellent condition with few edge chips, reverse near mint, 19" by 22".
$2,500+

Calso Supreme Gasoline
porcelain pump plate, excellent condition, 14" by 11".
$500+

Calso Supreme Gasoline
porcelain pump plate, excellent condition, 12" by 15".
$425+

Calso Supreme Gasoline
porcelain pump plate, very good condition, chips at mounting holes, 12" diameter.
$225+

Capitol Cylinder Oil
barrel label, Standard Oil Company, excellent condition, framed, 15" diameter.
$200+

Caution
single-sided porcelain plate, very good condition, 14" by 10".
$90+

Chevron
cardboard display, framed, 20" by 39".
$250+

Chevron Supreme
single-sided porcelain sign with lip on top, excellent condition, chip at bottom mounting hole, 5" by 12".
$80+

Chevron
single-sided tin sign, good condition, some edge flaking around mounting holes, 7 1/2" diameter.

$300+

Chevron Aviation Fuel
single-sided porcelain pricer, near mint, 8" by 11".

$300+

Chevron Aviation Fuels
single-sided porcelain die-cut sign, excellent condition-plus, 60" by 48".

$3,000+

Chevron Aviation Gasoline
porcelain pump plate, near mint-plus, 12" diameter.

$2,400+

Chevron Aviation Gasoline
single-sided porcelain sign, near mint-plus, 22" diameter.

$2,700+

Chevron Aviation Gasoline
porcelain pump plate, excellent condition, dime-size chip at upper mounting hole, 15" by 12".

$2,700+

Chevron Aviation Gasoline
single-sided porcelain sign, near mint, 22" by 18".

$1,400+

Chevron Credit Cards
double-sided porcelain sign with hallmark, excellent condition, 43" by 30".

$875+

Chevron Credit Cards Accepted
double-sided porcelain sign, excellent condition-plus, 33" diameter.

$450+

Chevron Diesel Fuel
porcelain pump plate with hallmark, excellent condition, small edge chips, 15" by 12".

$1,800+

Chevron Free Skypower Gliders
window poster, excellent condition, framed, 42" by 32".

$75+

Chevron Garage
single-sided porcelain beveled edge sign, good condition, four quarter-size chips in field, 14" by 84".

$1,000+

Chevron Gasoline
double-sided porcelain sign, excellent condition, few small chips in field, 33" diameter, rare.

$1,100+

Chevron Gasoline
porcelain pump plate with hallmark, near mint, 15" by 12".

$1,600+

Chevron Gasoline
porcelain pump plate, excellent condition, chips around bottom mounting holes, 12" diameter.

$775+

Chevron Gasoline
(marine) double-sided porcelain sign, good condition, large repair at bottom, clear coated, 12" diameter.

$500+

Chevron Gas Station
double-sided porcelain sign, poor to fair condition, 48" by 60".

$350+

Chevron Gas Station
neon sign, good condition, seven quarter-size chips touched up, original neon and can, 46" by 66".

$2,500+

Chevron Gas Station
single-sided porcelain self-framed sign, excellent condition, nickel-size chip in middle of field and along left side, 45" by 65".

$1,000+

Chevron Men and Women
restroom single-sided porcelain signs, near mint, 3" by 10", and 3" by 14".

$400+ pair

Chevron National Credit Cards Accepted
double-sided porcelain sign, very good condition, chip in upper left, 18" by 24".

$375+

Chevron Standard Dealer
single-sided porcelain die-cut sign, good condition, 72" by 48".

$850+

Chevron Standard Heating Oils
single-sided porcelain die-cut pump plate, excellent condition, 14" by 10".

$400+

Chevron Standard Heating Oils
single-sided porcelain die-cut sign, excellent condition, few chips, 60" by 48".

$425+

Chevron Supreme Gasoline
A-38 ad glass, fair to good condition, some fading.

$100+

Chevron Supreme Gasoline
single-sided Masonite sign, fair condition, wear to bottom, 24" diameter.

$275+

Chevron Supreme Gasoline
porcelain pump plate with hallmark, near mint,
15" by 12".

$1,900+

Chevron Supreme Gasoline
single-sided tin sign with hallmark, very good
condition, minor wear in field, 14" by 11".

$350+

Chevron Supreme Gasoline
porcelain pump plate, fair to good condition, chips
around edge, dated 1946, 12" diameter.

$300+

Chevron Supreme Gasoline
single-sided tin sign, fair to good condition, minor
paint loss on bottom edge, 24" diameter.

$2,600+

Chevron Supreme Gasoline
single-sided tin sign, fair to good condition, spotting in upper section, 24" diameter.

$200+

Chevron Supreme Gasoline
Masonite taxi cab tire sign, excellent condition,
18" diameter.

$150+

Cities Service Oils
single-sided porcelain lubster sign, excellent condition-plus, small stains in field, 10" diameter.

$700+

Col-Tex Gasoline
with Ethyl logo, near mint, 10" diameter.

$400+

Conoco Gasoline
with Ethyl logo double-sided porcelain sign,
display side poor to fair condition, reverse very
bad, 30" diameter.

$400+

Conoco Gasoline
with Minuteman double-sided porcelain sign, fair condition, several touched-up areas, 25" diameter.
$1,600+

Conoco Gasoline
with Minuteman double-sided porcelain sign, one side professionally restored, other side with numerous touch-ups and scratches, 30" diameter.
$1,150+

Conoco Ladies
restroom tin flange sign, excellent condition-plus, 5" by 10".
$100+

Conoco Ladies and Men
tin flange signs, excellent condition, each 5" by 10".

$200+ pair

Conoco Men
Rest Room porcelain flange sign, excellent condition, chips on flange, 10" by 10".
$550+

Conoco Men
restroom tin flange sign, excellent condition, light wear, 5" by 10".
$125+

Conoco Motor Oil
double-sided porcelain sign with Minute Man, display side very good condition with light wear to field, dime-size chips around mounting holes, more wear to reverse, slightly warped, 18" by 28".
$5,000+

Conoco Rest Rooms
tin flange sign, excellent condition-plus, 5" by 10".

$240+

Conoco
single-sided porcelain sign Danger Gas Line, fair to good condition, has had some touchup, 8" by 15".

$70+

Conoco
single-sided porcelain sign Do Not Oil While in Motion, fair to good condition, has some repair, 8" by 15".

$140+

Conoco Super Motor Oil
double-sided porcelain sign, fair condition, 30" by 37".

$125+

Conoco
truck door (early green outline) single-sided porcelain sign, excellent condition, one chip at top mounting hole, 11" diameter.

$350+

Cresyl Regular
porcelain pump plate, excellent condition-plus, light scuff in field, 10 1/2" by 11".

$625+

Crown Gasoline
(Kentucky) porcelain flange, fair condition, display side has overall wear, reverse fair to good, 26" by 26".
$1,500+

(The) Crystal-Flash Line
single-sided porcelain, good condition with numerous edge chips, 47" by 99".
$2,250+

Deep Rock
restroom creed single-sided porcelain sign, excellent condition, chipping along bottom edge, 10" square.
$800+

Derby Men
restroom tin flange sign, near mint, 6" by 13".
$400+

Derby Women
restroom tin flange sign, near mint, 6" by 13".
$450+

Dixie
tin pump plate sign, good condition, with significant wear, 24" by 13".
$90+

Douglas Aviation Regular
single-sided tin pump sign, near mint, 18" by 12 1/2".

$1,500+

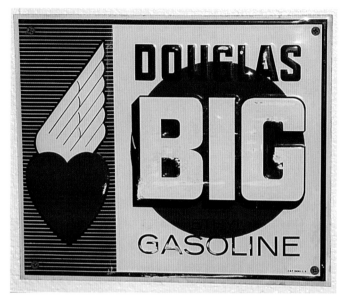

Douglas BIG Gasoline
single-sided tin embossed pump sign, very good condition, wear in center of field, 10" by 12".

$650+

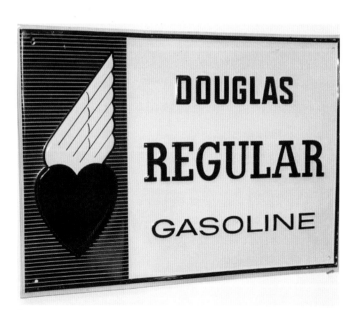

Douglas Regular Gasoline
embossed single-sided tin sign, near mint, new old stock, 10" by 14".

$550+

Dri-Powr
single-sided tin sign, excellent condition, 11 1/2" by 17".

$175+

En-Ar-Co Free Road Maps
(with boy) double-sided tin sign, dated 1937,
excellent condition with light scratches on display
side, reverse good with more scratches.

$300+

Dynafuel
die-cut single-sided porcelain pump plate, very good condition, chips along edges, 8" by 12".

$175+

Esso Elephant Kerosene
single-sided porcelain sign, poor to fair condition,
significant wear overall, 24" by 12".

$90+

Esso
double-sided porcelain metal-framed oval sign, very good condition, 26" by 38".

$650+

Esso Elephant Kerosene
single-sided porcelain sign, excellent condition
with small chips around mounting hole, 24" by
12".

$525+

Esso Motor Oil
double-sided tin sign, excellent condition, some chipping and rust, 10" by 18".

$175+

Esso Oil Drop Girl
die-cut single-sided tin sign, dated 1965, near
mint, 15" by 5".

$450+

Esso Uniflo Motor Oil
single-sided tin sign, very good condition, 10 1/2" by 17 1/2".

$130+

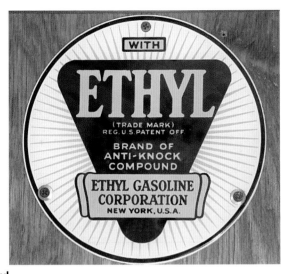

Ethyl
sunburst logo single-sided porcelain sign, excellent condition, 8" diameter.

$30+

Eureka Harness Oil
Standard Oil Indiana, single-sided tin with embossed horses, good condition, surface rust around edges, extra holes in field, minor wear, 13 1/2" by 19 1/2".

$475+

Fill-em' Fast Gasoline
porcelain pump plate, near mint, 9 1/2" by 15".

$200+

Fina Caution
restroom single-sided porcelain sign, near mint, 4 1/2" by 6".

$350+

Flamo Ask Us
single-sided porcelain sign, Standard Oil of California, near mint, small chip in field, 18" by 14".

$250+

Flamo
embossed tin tacker, excellent condition, slight rust at lower right corner, 9" by 6".

$100+

Flamo Gas-Equipped Cabins
single-sided porcelain sign, neon added, excellent condition, two quarter-size chips along edge, 30" by 60".

$2,300+

Flying A
die-cut porcelain pump plate, near mint, new old stock, 9" by 13 1/2".

$1,000+

Flying A Gasoline
double-sided tin sign with pipe frame, poor condition, 48" by 36".

$50+

Flying A Gasoline
porcelain pump plate, near mint, new old stock, 10" diameter.

$600+

Flying A Super Extra
porcelain pump plate, near mint, new old stock, 10" diameter.

$800+

Fyre-Drop
porcelain pump plate, fair to good condition with chipping around mounting holes, 10" diameter.

No established value

General Petroleum
2nd Annual Employees Picnic poster, fair to good condition, faded, 23" by 25".

$125+

The term "winter-front" requires some explanation for those drivers who don't have to deal with subfreezing temperatures. A winter-front is simply a windscreen mounted in a vehicle's grille to block the passage of cold air to the engine compartment, allowing the compartment to stay warmer, and heat the vehicle's interior quicker. The first winter-fronts were cut from old cardboard or wood boxes, until someone came up with the bright idea to produce examples with advertising. As you might expect, the nature of their use contributed to rapid disintegration, and most were ruined within months of being installed. Winter-fronts evolved into sturdier screens made of plastic or Naugahyde, but early examples with advertising can be highly prized.

General Gasoline
hand-painted signs, may be from flatbed truck, each 26" by 30".
$150+ pair

General Gasoline
winter-fronts, both fair condition, some damage.
$150+ pair

Gilmore No Smoking
double-sided porcelain sign, display side excellent condition with minor edge chipping, reverse very good with chip in field, chipping and rust on bottom edge, 6" by 36".
$4,750+

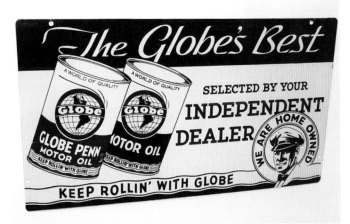

Globe's Best Motor Oil
double-sided tin sign, near mint, 12" by 21 1/2".
$950+

Globe Gasoline
double-sided tin sign, with original hangers, 42" diameter.
$2,500

Gloco Super Ethyl
die-cut porcelain pump plate, near mint, 9 1/2"
by 15".

$600+

Golden Eagle
porcelain pump plate, good condition, has
scratches in field, 13" square.

$500+

Golden Nugget Gasoline
porcelain pump plate, near mint, 10 1/2" diameter.

$1,300+

Golden West Oil Company
porcelain pump plate, new old stock.

$900+

Grizzly Gasoline
(Dubbs Cracked) Watch Your Miles double-sided tin sign, display side good
condition, light wear and fading at bottom, extremely rare, 36" by 24".

$3,500+

Good Gulf
porcelain pump plate, near mint, 10 1/2" diameter.

$110+

Grizzly Gasoline
(Dubbs Cracked) porcelain pump plate, excellent condition and gloss, 2" chip along edge, 12" diameter.

$5,750+

Gulf Aviation Products
single-sided porcelain sign, good condition, 45" by 70".

$2,700+

Gulf
backlit sign, working condition, 20" diameter.

$200+

Gulf
three variations of single-sided tin "lighthouse" signs, with wooden frames added later, each 29" by 61", 11 different versions, late 1920s.

$1,500+ each

Gulf Super No-Nox
porcelain pump plate, near mint, 9" by 11".

$100+

Gulf, De Luxe and Wow Gas
cardboard winter-fronts, fair condition or less.

$130+ all

Gulf
Mona Motor, Cities Service and Marine Gas cardboard winter-fronts, fair to good condition or less.

$130+ all

Gulftane
porcelain pump plate, near mint, 8 1/2" by 11".

$60+

Hancock Gasoline
cardboard winter-front, fair condition, some water staining.

$175+

Hancock Gasoline
(early rooster) porcelain pump plate, very good condition with repaired quarter-size hole below "A" in Hancock, 12" diameter.

$3,100+

Hancock No Smoking
double-sided porcelain sign, very good condition, small chips in field and slight bend, reverse good with more chips, 6" by 30".

$3,500+

Havoline Motor Oil
single-sided porcelain sign, near mint, dated 1941, 11" by 21 1/2".

$350+

Havoline
Waukee Oil, Koolmotor and Cities Service cardboard winter-fronts, fair condition or less.

$160+ all

Hemphill
wooden die-cut delivery truck, very good condition, 68" by 24".

$275+

Home-Clean Rest Rooms
double-sided tin sign, very good condition, 14" by 17".

$100+

Humble
restroom creed single-sided porcelain sign, near mint, 9" by 7".

$500+

Humble Top Rated Rest Rooms
double-sided porcelain sign, dated 1964, excellent condition, 30" by 30".

$300+

Husky Hi Power
porcelain pump plate, near mint, 12" square.

$600+

Husky Service
double-sided porcelain die-cut sign, good condition, large chips and re-drilled holes at top and small chips in field, light scratches, larger chips on reverse, 48" by 42".

$4,250+

Husky Tri-Power
porcelain pump plate, near mint, 12" square.

$1,600+

Imperial Refineries
with Ethyl logo porcelain pump plate, excellent condition-plus, small chip on left edge.

$950+

Indian Gasoline
curved porcelain pump plate, near mint, dated 1940, 18" by 10 1/2".

$425+

Indian Motorcycle Motor Oil
bevel-edge single-sided tin easel sign, excellent condition-plus, light wear, glossy, 9 1/2" by 13".

$1,600+

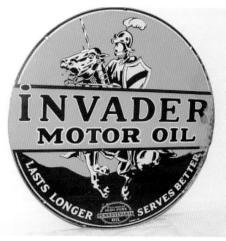

Invader Motor Oil
(with knight) double-sided tin sign, display side very good condition, some paint loss, reverse good with more paint loss, rare, 24" diameter.

$1,400+

Invader Motor Oil
single-sided tin sign, frame edge, new old stock, 58" by 34".

$1,800

ISO-VIS
double-sided porcelain sign, poor condition, fading and large crease at top, 30" diameter.

$125+

ISO-VIS
porcelain Lubster sign, excellent condition, minor edge chips, 7" diameter.

$275+

ISO-VIS D Motor Oil
single-sided porcelain self-framed sign, near mint, 60" by 16".

$400+

Johnson Oils Gasolene
Time Tells cardboard winter-front, excellent condition.

$250+

Porcelain signs
in Rich Gannon's collection, including a 30" Johnson Gasolene "Time Tells" double-sided sign with Ethyl logo, very good condition. (Collector Tip: The rarest version of the Johnson "Time Tells" sign includes an image of an hourglass.)

Johnson sign, $3,200+

Kendall The 2000 Mile Oil
curved single-sided porcelain sign, very good condition and gloss, two quarter-size chips in field, chip at left mounting hole, 30" by 20".

$3,700+

Keynoil
"A" for Fords single-sided tin sign, near mint.

$1,500

Keynoil
(White Eagle) double-sided porcelain oval sign, fair to good condition, 20" by 28".

$600+

Keystone Powerfuel
porcelain pump plate, excellent condition, dated 1955, 14" by 12".

$650+

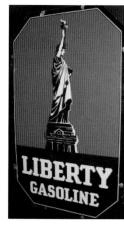

Liberty Gasoline
double-sided porcelain die-cut sign, display side very good condition, reverse good, touched-up chips around edge, 48" by 30".

$6,250+

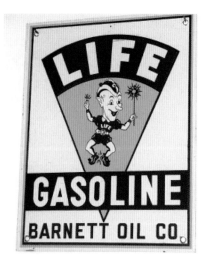

Life Gasoline
tin pump plate sign, rare, 10" by 8".

$1,300+

Lion Head Motor Oil
single-sided tin, 29" by 11 3/4". (Beware of reproductions.)

$500+

Lion Monsanto
single-sided tin pump plate sign, excellent condition, 24" by 14".

$110+

Magnolia Gasoline
for sale here double-sided porcelain sign, excellent condition-plus, light scratches on reverse, 30" diameter.

$2,700+

Magnolia Pegasus
single-sided porcelain sign, good condition, 16" by 27".

$350+

Malco
porcelain pump plate, near mint, has a few very light scratches, 12" diameter.

$1,300+

Mars Ethyl
single-sided porcelain pump plate, near mint, 17" by 14".

$550+

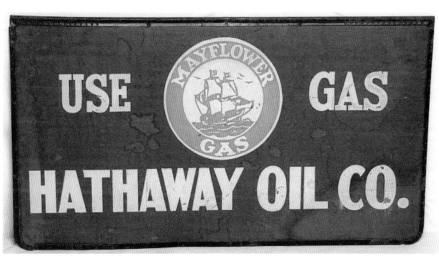

Mayflower Gas
cardboard winter-front, good condition.

$60+

Mica Axle Grease
single-sided tin embossed tacker, fair to good condition, wrinkled, 4 1/2" by 19 1/2".

$175+

Merit Auto Oil
round barrel label, Standard Oil (Kentucky), good condition, framed, 15" diameter.

$50+

Mica Axle Grease
single-sided tin tacker, good condition, light wear and fading, 4 1/2" by 19 1/2".

$100+

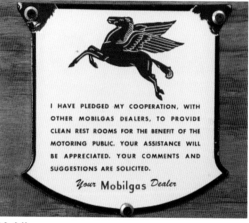

Mobil
(black border) Restroom pledge single-sided porcelain shield sign, near mint, 8" by 8".

$1,000+

Mobil
(blue border) Restroom pledge single-sided porcelain shield sign, very good condition, chips at top mounting holes, 8" by 8".

$400+

Mobil Distributor
single-sided porcelain sign, fair to good condition, 28" by 60".

$100+

Mobiloil Gargoyle
single-sided porcelain sign, red and black design on top and bottom edge, fair to good condition, chips around mounting holes, 22 1/2" by 15".

$550+

Mobilgas
cardboard die-cut winter-front and Mobil Pegasus cardboard winter-front, both good condition.

$110+ pair

Mobilgas
neon single-sided porcelain sign, poor condition, 24" by 108".

$1,900+

Mobilgas/Mobiloil
single-sided tin self-framed sign, good condition, 24" by 72".

$200+

Mobilgas
die-cut porcelain pump plate, near mint, 13" by 12 1/2".

$525+

Mobilgas
(East Coast) pledge shield, excellent condition, 7 1/2" by 8".

$650+

Mobilgas New Spring
cloth banner with lamb, good condition.

$125+

Mobilgas Pegasus
identification hanging sign, dated 1932, good condition, 48" by 48".

$700+

Mobilgas Pegasus
"Just Ahead" single-sided tin embossed self-framed sign, fair to good condition, 58" by 45".

$900+

Mobilgas
"Restroom Pledge Plate" single-sided porcelain sign, near mint, new old stock, 9 1/2" by 7".

$650+

Mobilgas Special
die-cut porcelain pump plate, dated 1951, with blue border, near mint.

$250+

Mobilgas Special Gasoline
single-sided porcelain pump plate with black border, very good condition, dime-size chip on Pegasus, 12" by 12".

$150+

Mobilgas Special
single-sided porcelain pump plate, dated 1954, very good condition, 12" by 12".

$100+

Mobilgas
(West Coast) pledge shield, excellent condition, 7 1/2" by 8".

$550+

Mobil Ladies Rest Room
tin flange sign, dated 1941, good condition, 10" by 19".

$575+

Mobilubrication
plywood single-sided sign, fair to good condition, 38" by 30".

$75+

Mobil-gloss
cleaner and polish single-sided tin sign, with paint loss at bottom, scratches and "ambering" (yellowing), 48" by 24".

$900+

Mobil-gloss
single-sided tin die-cut sign, very good condition, 48" by 24".

$1,400+

Mobilgas
single-sided porcelain self-framed sign, good condition with chips along edge, 10" by 108".

$1,000+

MobiLubrication Certified
single-sided tin die-cut wood-framed sign, fair condition, 33" by 132".

$800+

MobiLubrication
Socony-Vacuum SS Masonite sign, wood frame, very good condition with holes, 36" by 108".

$800+

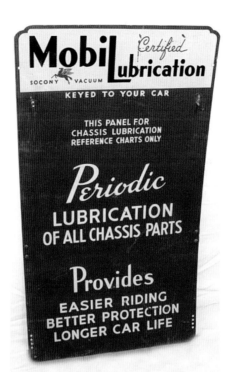

MobiLubrication
single-sided tin chart, fair condition, 47" by 27".
$200+

Mobiloil Arctic Gargoyle
porcelain lubster sign, display side excellent condition, reverse good with large chip and crazing.
$275+

Mobiloil Gargoyle
single-sided tin embossed framed sign, near mint,
19" by 14 1/2".
$550+

Mobiloil
single-sided tin sign with original wood frame,
15" by 60".
$1,000

Mobiloil Lubrication Chart
single-sided porcelain sign, near mint condition,
29" by 36".
No established value

Mobiloil Gargoyle
Drain Out Winter leather and cardboard tire
cover, fair condition, 31" diameter.
$950+

Mobil Pegasus
single-sided porcelain sign, good condition, chips, 14 1/2" by 14".

$110+

Mobiloil
framed single-sided tin vertical sign, fair condition, 61" by 16".

$250+

Mobiloil
single-sided porcelain framed sign, fair to good condition, 60" by 16".

$525+

Mobil Pegasus
porcelain die-cut sign, poor to fair condition, 60" by 90".

$650+

Mobiloil Pegasus
single-sided porcelain sign, very good condition, chips and touch-ups, 22" by 15".

$250+

Mobiloi
single-sided porcelain pump plate, dated 1946, very good condition, chip in lower right, 12" by 12".

$300+

Mobiloil
single-sided porcelain sign (French), good condition, 11" by 19".

$110+

Mobiloil Service
single-sided neon sign, good condition with some edge chips, 32" by 32".

$2,750+

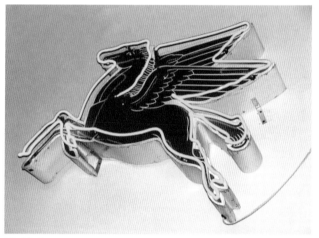

Mobil Pegasus
neon die-cut porcelain single-sided sign, good condition with touchups, 40" by 40".

$2,000+

Mobil Pegasus
single-sided porcelain sign, black border, fair to good condition with chips and fading, 24" by 36".

$300+

Mobil
single-sided porcelain sign, good condition, 31" by 63".

$400+

Mobil
single-sided porcelain sign, fair condition, 28" by 60".

$50+

Mobil
die-cut double-sided porcelain identification sign, excellent condition, 41" by 82".

$450+

Mobil Pegasus
single-sided tin pump plate with decal, good condition, 12" by 12".

$110+

Mobil Pegasus
painted porcelain disk, fair to good condition, worn, 12" diameter.

$60+

Mobil Pegasus
single-sided porcelain sign, with Marine White decal, good condition, has chips around both center mounting holes, 14" by 15".

$100+

Mobil Pegasus
single-sided porcelain sign, good condition, large chip on top and small chips around edges, 20" by 22".

$175+

Mobil Restroom
Locked for Your Protection single-sided tin sign, excellent condition, light wear, 3 1/2" by 9".

$175+

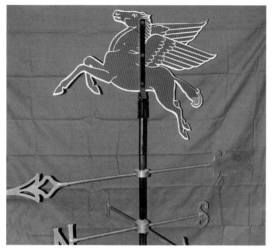

Mobil Tires
with Pegasus single-sided tin sign, good condition, 24" by 108".

$500+

Mona Motor Oil
Authorized Dealer single-sided tin sign, poor to fair condition, 11" by 35".

$100+

Mobil Pegasus
weathervane double-sided porcelain sign, excellent condition, 44" by 31".

$2,900+

Moore's Supreme
with Ethyl logo single-sided porcelain sign, near mint, 15" by 10".

$725+

Moore's Supreme Regular
logo single-sided porcelain sign, near mint, 15" by 10".

$750+

Motul Motor Oils
single-sided porcelain sign, excellent condition, 25" square.

$200+

Nervic Oil
single-sided tin sign, excellent condition, minor edge wear, 19" by 13".

$425+

Nofrez
.20 per QT. double-sided porcelain sign, near mint, 10" by 18".

$250+

Oilzum Motor Oil
die-cut single-sided tin sign, dated 1949, excellent condition, 20" by 19".

$425+

Oilzum
double-sided porcelain sign, 24" diameter.

$4,000

Pan-Am Clean Restrooms Award
double-sided porcelain die-cut sign, display side excellent condition, reverse very good with chip and crazing, 50" by 13".

$4,100+

Oronite Cleaning Fluid
cardboard poster, very good condition, wear at corners, framed, 29" by 23".

$75+

Pan-Am Motor Oils
single-sided porcelain Lubster sign, excellent condition, 15" diameter.

$1,150+

Pan-Am Quality Gasoline
porcelain pump plate, dated 1955, excellent condition-plus.

$275+

Pan-Am
single-sided porcelain pump plate, good condition, chips and field wear, 17" by 13".

$150+

Parabase Motor Oil
double-sided tin sign, display side has been restored, 12" by 30".

$225+

Paraland
Motor Oil/Gasoline double-sided porcelain sign, 5 feet wide.

$2,500+

Pearl Oil Kerosene
die-cut tin flange with red label, near mint, 18" by 11".

$1,900+

Pearl Oil Kerosene
tin flange with King of Kerosene, very good to excellent condition, light wear, 8" by 12".

$150+

Pearl Oil Kerosene
die-cut flange, 1947 Standard Oil Company, blue label, near mint, 19" by 12".

$2,600+

Pearl Oil Kerosene
tin flange sign, Standard Oil of California, dated 1947, display side good condition with paint loss bottom edge, reverse fair, 19" by 12".

$450+

Penn-Drake Motor Oil
single-sided tin, 28" by 9 1/2".

$400

PennField Motor Oils
single-sided tin, 19 1/2" by 13 1/2".

$400

Pennsylvania Consumers Oil Co.
single-sided tin, 17 1/2" by 7 3/4".

$250

Penn-Union
single-sided tin sign.

$550

Pennzoil Ask For It
double-sided tin curb sign, 36" by 24".

$30+

Pennzoil
double-sided tin hanging sign with hanger, display side excellent condition,
reverse good, dated 1947, 18" by 30".

$200+

Pennzoil We Are Bonded
double-sided tin sign, good condition, 10 1/2" by 13 1/2".

$100+

Perfection Kerosene
tin flange, Standard Oil, excellent condition, 14" by 18".

$550+

Perfection Oil
tin over cardboard sign, excellent condition, minor dents, small paint scuff, framed, 13" by 19".

$850+

Penn Motor Oil
Amoco and Derby cardboard winter-fronts, good condition or less.

$120+ all

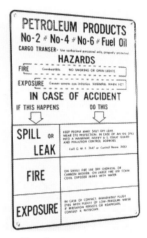

Petroleum Products
"In Case of Accident" single-sided porcelain sign, near mint, 18" by 12".

$50+

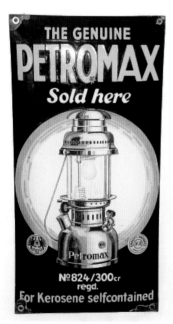

Petromax Sold Here
single-sided porcelain domed sign, very good condition, dime-size chip in field, chips at mounting holes, 25" by 13".

$350+

Phillips 66
Go With the Gasoline that Won The West single-sided tin sign, good condition with some field wear, 16" by 15 1/2".

$325+

Phillips 66
double-sided porcelain shield, dated 1966, fair to good condition with several large chips, 48" by 48".

$275+

Phillips 66
double-sided porcelain shield, excellent condition,
29" by 29".

$450+

Pierce Pennant Motor Oil
cardboard winter-fronts, each very good condition.

$225+ pair

Polarine Consult Chart
tin flange, very good condition, 14" by 18".

$500+

Polarine Made in Five Grades
double-sided porcelain triangle sign, fair condition, overall wear and chips around edges, 24" by 24".

$500+

Polarine Motor Oil
and Gasoline double-sided porcelain sign, very good condition, 30" diameter.

$650+

Polarine Motor Car Oil
embossed single-sided tin sign, excellent condition-plus, 9" by 20".

$550+

Polarine Motor Car Oil
for Sale Here single-sided tin sign, good to excellent condition, 9" by 18 1/2".

$2,300+

Polarine Motor Oil
and Greases tin flange, fair to good condition, scratches and wear, 9" by 18".
$150+

Polarine Motor Oils
Standard Oil of Nebraska, porcelain flange, display side poor to fair condition, chips around edges, five dime-size chips in field, staining, reverse very poor, faded, small hole next to flange, 18" by 22".
$425+

Polarine Oil & Greases
for Motor Cars and Motor Boats single-sided tin sign, excellent condition, two light wrinkles, 4 1/2" by 19 1/2".
$450+

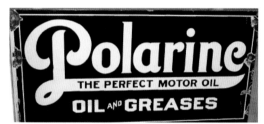

Polarine Oil and Greases
porcelain flange, good condition with edge chips and four holes drilled in edge, 12" by 24".
$700+

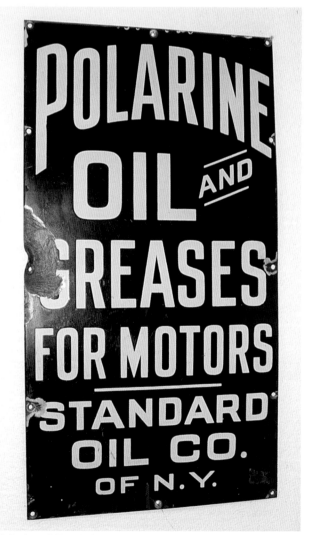

Polarine Oil Greases for Motors
with Socony logo double-sided porcelain sign, display side very good condition with edge chips and light wear, reverse with two quarter-size chips and fading, 15" by 24".
$700+

Polarine Oil and Greases for Motors
single-sided porcelain sign, Standard Oil Co. N.Y., fair condition, large chipped area middle left edge, 18" by 22".
$300+

Polarine Oils Greases
Sold Here porcelain flange, display side excellent condition, small edge chips, reverse very good with quarter-size chip on edge, 15" by 26".

$425+

Polarine
The Standard Oil for Motor Cars porcelain flange, display side fair to good condition, edge chips and wear in field, reverse poor to fair with edge chips and fading, 12" by 24".

$650+

Power-lube Motor Oil
double-sided porcelain sign, near mint with minor wear and fading, 20" by 28". (Beware of reproductions, which are a lighter blue and don't have grommets around the mounting holes.)

$1,800-$2,500

Polarine
porcelain Lubster sign, excellent condition, 7" diameter.

$400+

Pure Firebird Regular
plastic pump plate, good condition, some warping.

$60+

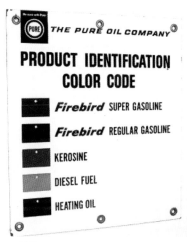

Pure Oil
"Product Identification Color Code" single-sided porcelain sign, excellent condition, 17" by 15".

$100+

Pure Ok'd Clean Rest Rooms
double-sided porcelain sign, excellent condition
with chips around mounting holes, 26" by 18".

$275+

Pure-Pep Be sure with Pure
porcelain pump plate, excellent condition, one
small chip, 12" by 10".

$110+

Pure-Pep Regular
single-sided porcelain sign, excellent condition,
12" by 10".

$160+

Pure Pep
single-sided porcelain sign, good condition, large
chip around mounting hole, 15" diameter.

$525+

Pure "Please Ask Attendant"
single-sided porcelain sign, mint condition, 6" by 11".

$225+

Pure Tiolene Motor Oil
tin flange sign, near mint, 15" by 20".

$650+

Pure Premium
porcelain pump plate, dated 1948, excellent condition-plus, 12" by 10".

$90+

Pure Puritan Motor Oil
decal on glass, 9 1/2" by 12".

$10+

Pure Tiolene
double-sided porcelain sign, excellent condition, some scratches.

$825+

Pure Oil
cardboard winter-fronts, each good condition.

$160+ all

Pyroil
single-sided tin vertical self-framed sign, fair condition, 56" by 15".

$375+

Quaker State Racing Oil
single-sided tin sign.

$70+

Red Crown Gasoline
1925 framed poster, fair condition, with staining,
5 feet by 4 feet.

$190+

Red Crown Gasoline
chalk board pricer double-sided tin sign, fair condition, wear and
staining, 13" by 14".

$375+

Red Crown Gasoline
double-sided porcelain sign (black background),
poor condition, faded and overall wear, 30"
diameter.

$450+

Red Crown Gasoline
double-sided porcelain sign, good condition,
quarter-size chip in border, 30" diameter.

$450+

Red Crown Gasoline
double-sided porcelain sign, display side good,
reverse fair with chips and scratches, original
hardware, 30" diameter.

$900+

Red Crown Gasoline
double-sided porcelain sign, overall very poor to
poor, 30" diameter.

$325+

Red Crown Gasoline
double-sided porcelain sign, with Ethyl logo,
fair condition, five significant chips in field, 30"
diameter.

$500+

Red Crown Gasoline
GM Ethyl double-sided porcelain sign, professionally restored, 30" diameter.

$1,500+

Red Crown Gasoline
(Kentucky) die-cut porcelain flange, fair to good condition, large chips touched up in center of field, 26" by 26".

$800+

Red Crown Gasoline
(Nebraska) porcelain flange, near mint, reverse has factory blemish upper right corner, 18" by 22".

$2,500+

Red Crown Gasoline
painted metal curb sign, excellent condition, 30" diameter.

$650+

Red Crown The Gasoline of Quality
single-sided porcelain tank wagon sign, poor to fair condition, significant chipping and overall wear, 12" by 96".

$300+

Red Crown Gasoline
porcelain flange, excellent condition, 24" by 24".

$2,900+

Red Crown Gasoline
porcelain paddle sign, near mint, 8" by 11".

$1,550+

Red Crown Gasoline
porcelain paddle sign, near mint, 10" by 13".

$1,300+

Red Crown Gasoline
porcelain paddle sign, excellent condition, small chip bottom center, 14" by 17".

$1,000+

Red Crown Gasoline
Power Mileage single-sided porcelain sign, good condition, two large chips in field, edge chipping, 28" by 60".

$100+

Red Crown Gasoline
Scrip Accepted porcelain paddle sign, excellent condition, 12" by 13".

$1,600+

Red Crown Gasoline
single-sided porcelain sign, very good condition, small chip in field, 42" diameter.

$1,650+

Red Crown
Scrip Accepted double-sided porcelain paddle sign, display side good condition with quarter size chip, reverse fair to good with large chip, 12" by 13".

$525+

Red Crown Gasoline
single-sided porcelain truck sign, near mint, 12" by 14".

$2,900+

Red Crown Gasoline
tin flange (yellow background), display side very good condition, minor paint loss along edges, reverse damaged beyond repair, 19" by 26".

$650+

Red Crown Gasoline
Wild To Go winter-front, excellent condition, framed, 10" by 16".

$200+

Red Crown Gasoline Zerolene
double-sided porcelain, fair to good condition, chipping in fields and on edges, 42" diameter.

$4,000+

Red Crown
it's Purple...it's Powerful tin and cardboard truck topper, very good condition, 8" by 36" by 32".

$300+

Red Crown Stove Gasoline
single-sided tin tacker, excellent condition, some paint crazing, 6" by 20". (Collector Tip: "Tacker" refers to a small, lightweight single-sided tin sign that could be held in place with tacks.)

$550+

Red Crown
The Gasoline of Quality single-sided porcelain tank wagon sign, fair condition, edge chips and 2" chip in center of field, 11" by 72".

$250+

Red Crown
The Gasoline of Quality single-sided porcelain tank wagon sign, fair to good condition, large chips at mounting holes, 9" by 24".

$350+

Red Hat Motor Oil
lubster sign, fair to good condition, reverse very poor, 6 3/4" diameter.

$400+

Renown Engine Oil
barrel label, Standard Oil of Kentucky, excellent condition, framed, 15" diameter.

$100+

Republic
porcelain pump plate, excellent condition, small chips around edge, 11" by 12".

$250+

Richfield Ethyl
double-sided porcelain sign, excellent condition-plus, 25" diameter.

$4,750+

Richfield
restroom creed single-sided porcelain sign, near mint, 8" by 6".

$1,600+

Richfield Rich-Heat Heating Oil
single-sided porcelain sign, good condition, 21" square.

$250+

Richfield Solvent-Treated
single-sided tin sign, near mint, new old stock, dated 1946, 12" by 16".

$400+

Richfield Women
restroom single-sided porcelain dome sign, near mint, 3" by 10".

$900+

Richfield Men
restroom single-sided porcelain dome sign, near mint, 3" by 10".

$400+

Richfield
cardboard winter-fronts, both fair condition, some damage.

$400+ pair

Richlube
adjustable die-cut cardboard winter-front and Byrum Oil cardboard winter-front, poor to fair condition.

$60+ pair

Richlube
porcelain flange sign, excellent condition, 6" by 24".

$2,100+

Richlube Motor Oil
double-sided porcelain sign with race car, fair to good condition, silver-dollar size chips around mounting holes, 24" diameter.

$1,900+

Richlube Super HD
single-sided tin sign, excellent condition, 12" by 16".

$175+

Ritters Gasoline
porcelain pump plate, excellent condition, small touched up chip around bottom mounting hole.

$275+

Ritters Gasoline
single-sided porcelain sign, very good condition, touched up, 10" by 14".

$300+

Robert B. Doe Oil Field Service
single-sided porcelain truck sign, new old stock,
14" diameter.

$550+

Royal Daylight Oil
porcelain flange sign, fair condition, color fading and wear, 15" by 20".

$325+

Royal
die-cut porcelain pump plate, near mint, new old stock, 8 1/2" by
9 1/2".

$175+

Royal Triton Motor Oil
double-sided porcelain curb sign, in homemade
stand, excellent condition, 18" by 30".

$150+

RPM Aviation Oils
double-sided porcelain sign with hallmark, near
mint, 60" by 48".

$2,700+

RPM
cardboard spinner motorized display, good condition, minor damage along edge, 20" by 24".

$425+

RPM Motor Oil
1939 Walt Disney Mickey Mouse single-sided tin sign, poor condition, paint loss and staining in field, 24" diameter.

$1,250+

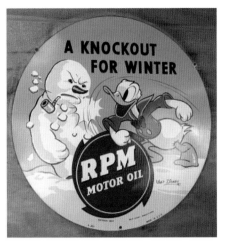

RPM Motor Oil
1940 Walt Disney Donald Duck sign, near mint, 24" diameter.

$7,000+

RPM Motor Oil
double-sided porcelain curb sign, very good condition, small chip in field at mounting hole, with original base, 27" diameter without base.

$600+

RPM Motor Oil
at Calso Stations single-sided tin embossed sign, good condition, minor paint loss and scratches in field, 24" by 36".

$225+

RPM Motor Oil
double-sided porcelain sign, display side good condition, significant chipping, reverse fair to good with chips in field, 30" diameter.

$200+

RPM Motor Oil
double-sided tin sign, good condition, 12" square.

$300+

RPM Motor Oil
double-sided tin sign with hallmark, excellent condition, minor scratch on right edge, 24" by 30".

$425+

RPM Motor Oil Heavy Duty
double-sided porcelain sign, excellent condition, two dime-size chips upper right, 33" diameter.

$650+

RPM Motor Oil
Lubster sign, decal over tin, very good condition,
6 1/2" by 6".

$15+

RPM Motor Oil
single-sided tin sign, good condition, minor
roughness around edge, 24" diameter.

$100+

RPM Motor Oil Thermo-Charged
die-cut porcelain flange, near mint, 22" by 22".

$1,300+

RPM Motor Oils and Lubricants
single-sided tin sign, excellent condition, 8" by 18".

$100+

RPM Motor Oils
double-sided tin sign, fair to good condition, overall wear, 6" by 16".

$100+

RPM Motor Oils
single-sided tin self-framed sign, excellent condition, 57" by 33".

$400+

RPM Supreme Motor Oil
half-round tin sign, excellent condition, 30" by
18".

$300+

RPM Thermo-Charged
Lubster sign, decal over tin, overall wear, 8" by 6".

$15+

RPM
single-sided porcelain sign with beveled edge on three sides, fair to good condition, chips on edge and in field, part of larger sign, 14" by 48".

$200+

Seaside Stop Smoking
double-sided porcelain sign, excellent condition, touched up around mounting holes, 6" by 36".

$2,250+

Sanitized Sterilseat Rest Rooms
double-sided porcelain sign, excellent condition, 18" by 24".

$125+

Seaside No Smoking
single-sided porcelain sign, neon added, near mint, 38" by 38".

$4,250+

Seaside
rolled-edge single-sided tin sign, 16" by 15", excellent condition.

$100+

Shamrock Trail Master Regular
porcelain pump plate, near mint, 12 1/2" by 10 1/2".

$225+

Shell Aeroshell
Lubricating Oil Stocked Here double-sided porcelain die-cut sign, very good condition, chips around edge, reverse has more chips along bottom edge, 15" by 28".

$1,700+

Shellane Bottled Gas Distributor
double-sided porcelain sign, excellent condition-plus, 20" by 30".

$475+

Shell Authorized Dealer
Credit Cards Accepted Here single-sided porcelain sign, very good condition, 18" by 48".

$450+

Shell Authorized Dealer
single-sided porcelain die-cut sign, with heavy metal frame, poor to fair condition, touched up, 18" by 26".

$850+

Shell
backlit clam on wooden frame, 24" diameter.

$175+

Shell
well number 226 single-sided porcelain sign, fair to good condition, both top corners repaired, 7" by 24".

$200+

Shell
double-sided porcelain well marker, good condition, with bullet hole, 12" by 28".

$25+

Shell
embossed clam porcelain neon sign, poor condition, neon broken, 42" by 36".

$900+

Shell
embossed plastic pump sign, excellent condition, 12" by 11".

$80+

Shell Gasoline
double-sided porcelain die-cut sign, dated 1929, fair condition, chips and field wear, 25" by 24".

$500+

Shell Gasoline
porcelain pump plate (red background), near mint, 12" by 12".

$2,600+

Shell Green Streak Gasoline
porcelain pump plate, near mint, 12" diameter.

$5,000+

Shell
(Golden) Motor Oil porcelain pump plate, very good condition, three drilled holes filed and touched up, 12" by 12".

$1,700+

Shell Home-Clean Rest Rooms
double-sided porcelain sign, very good condition, 22" by 15".

$375+

Shell Home-Clean Rest Room
Good Housekeeping Magazine single-sided porcelain sign, two chips over text, 7" diameter.

$100+

Shell Home-Clean Rest Rooms
(with comment cards) single-sided tin sign, excellent condition, light scratches, 12" by 9".

$350+

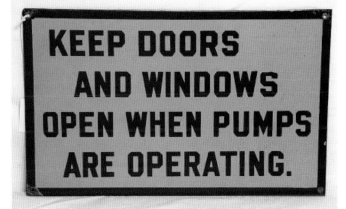

Shell
Keep Doors And Windows Open When Pumps Are Operating single-sided porcelain sign, good condition, quarter-size chip around bottom left mounting hole, 11" by 18".

$350+

Shell Substation
single-sided tin embossed sign, good condition with holes in field, 9" by 18".

$100+

Shell Ladies
restroom single-sided porcelain die-cut sign, near mint, 2" by 10".

$250+

Shell Gentlemen
restroom single-sided porcelain die-cut sign, near mint, 2" by 10".

$325+

Shellubrication
The Modern Upkeep Service single-sided porcelain sign, fair to good condition, chips in field and around mounting holes, 12" by 12".

$2,000+

Shell/Mobil Citrus Association
single-sided porcelain sign, poor to fair condition, 11" by 48".

$175+

Shell Notice
single-sided porcelain sign, excellent condition, quarter-size chip in bottom center, 16" by 30".

$325+

Shell Super-Shell Gasoline
porcelain pump plate, very good condition, quarter-size chip and small chips around mounting holes, 12" by 12".

$1,200+

Shell
porcelain letters, fair condition.

$525+ all

Shell Premium Gasoline
porcelain pump plate, excellent condition-plus, dime-size chip around bottom hole, 12" by 12".

$1,700+

Shell Notice
Smoking Absolutely Prohibited single-sided tin sign, poor to fair condition, with heavy wear, 16" by 23 1/2".

$200+

Shell
The Symbol of a Home-Clean Rest Room single-sided porcelain sign, excellent condition, chips at mounting holes, 10" diameter.

$200+

Shell Warning Pipeline
single-sided porcelain sign, fair condition, chips around center mounting holes, 8 1/2" by 10 1/2".

$120+

Shell
cardboard winter-fronts, each very good condition.

$60+ pair

Shell X-100 Motor Oil
double-sided tin curb sign, excellent condition, 35" by 26".

$650+

Shell
die-cut cardboard winter-fronts, one excellent condition, one good condition, with dust staining.

$90+ pair

Shell
cardboard winter-fronts, each very good condition.

$70+ all

Signal
die-cut single-sided porcelain truck sign, near mint, 5" by 28".

$1,400+

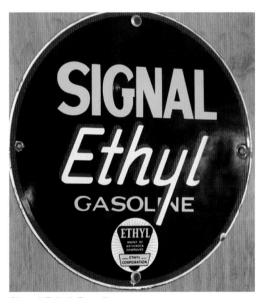

Signal Ethyl Gasoline
porcelain pump plate, excellent condition, light edge chips, 12" diameter.

$1,000+

Signal Gas Ahead
single-sided tin die-cut sign with stop light, excellent condition, rare, 24" by 22".

$4,000+

Signal Gasoline
porcelain pump plate with stoplight, excellent condition, 12" diameter.

$2,000+

Signal Products
cardboard winter-front, excellent condition.

$110+

Sinclair Credit Cards Honored
double-sided porcelain sign, display side excellent condition, reverse very good with chip on edge, 14" by 23".

$150+

Sinclair Identification
double-sided porcelain sign, poor condition, 60" by 96".

$100+

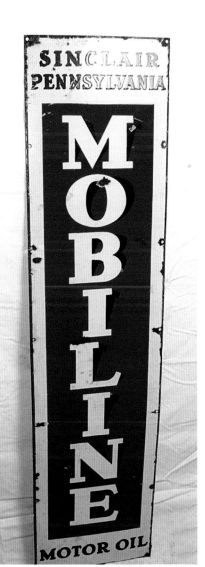

Sinclair Opaline Motor Oil
Lubster single-sided porcelain sign, very good condition, one scuff mark on each side, good gloss, 11" diameter.

$775+

Sinclair Pennsylvania
(black dinosaur) porcelain pump plate, fair to good condition, with repaired quarter-size chip in center, minor edge wear, 11" diameter.

$800+

Sinclair Mobiline Motor Oil
single-sided porcelain vertical sign, poor condition, 60" by 15".

$475+

Sinclair Opaline Motor Oil
single-sided tin sign, excellent condition, 12" by 20".

$575+

Skylark Aviation Grade Gasoline
neon sign, with plane skywriting, replaced neon and housing (or as collectors call it, the "can"), 42" by 66".

$8,000+

Sinclair
truck single-sided porcelain sign, near mint, 9" by 12".

$500+

S.O. Automotive Diesel Fuel
porcelain pump plate with hallmark, near mint-plus, 15" by 12".

$2,300+

Socony Aircraft Oil
No.1 Medium porcelain die-cut lubster sign, very good condition, minor edge chips, 12" by 8".

$450+

Socony Aircraft Oil
No. 2 Heavy Medium porcelain die-cut lubster sign, very good condition, minor edge chips, 12" by 8".

$425+

Socony Aircraft Oil
No. 3 Special Heavy porcelain die-cut lubster sign, excellent condition, 12" by 8".

$2,100+

Socony Aircraft Oil
No. 4 Super Heavy porcelain die-cut lubster sign, good condition, minor wear, 12" by 8".

$450+

Socony
die-cut double-sided porcelain Asian sign, good condition, edge chipping, 24" by 18".

$725+

Socony Air-Craft Oils
single-sided porcelain sign, excellent condition, few chips on right edge, scrape on bottom, 20" by 30".

$2,400+

Socony Liquid Gloss
tin over cardboard sign, near mint, 6" by 9".

$325+

Socony Lubricant
(pressure gun grease) double-sided porcelain sign, fair condition, nickel-size chips around mounting holes, crazing, 18" by 30".

$375+

Socony Motor Oil
porcelain flange, display side good condition, three chips, reverse has three quarter-size chips, 15" by 30".

$200+

Socony Motor Oil
Medium porcelain lubster sign, very good condition, minor edge chips, 12" by 8".

$325+

Socony Motor Gasoline
die-cut porcelain flange, very good to excellent condition, 24" by 20".

$1,600+

Socony Motor Oil
Extra Heavy porcelain lubster sign, excellent condition, 9 1/2" by 8".

$375+

Socony Parabase Motor Oil
single-sided porcelain sign, near mint, 6" by 9".

$750+

Socony Motor Oil
single-sided porcelain sign, very good condition, quarter-size chip lower right corner.

$475+

Socony Motor Oil
single-sided porcelain, good condition, dime-size chips at mounting holes and scratches in field, 14" by 10".

$250+

Socony Motor Oils
single-sided porcelain sign, very good condition, minor edge chips, 15" diameter.

$575+

Socony Motor Oils
single-sided porcelain curved pump sign, good condition, damage on bottom, 15" by 14".

$220+

Socony Parabase Motor Oil
Heavy porcelain lubster sign, good condition, edge chips and some facing, 12" by 8".

$300+

Socony Parabase Motor Oil
Medium porcelain lubster sign, very good condition, minor edge chips, 12" by 8".

$375+

Socony Safety First
domed tin sign, excellent condition, 8 1/2" diameter.

$350+

Socony-Vacuum
Credit Cards Honored Here double-sided porcelain sign, good condition with scratch and touchup, 14" by 20".

$250+

Socony Vacuum Marine Products
sign with Pegasus, 12" by 11 1/2", very good condition.

$500+

Sohio Gasoline High Test
double-sided porcelain sign, with Ethyl logo, fair to go5od condition, quarter-size chips in field, edge chips, wear in field, 26" by 30".

$600+

Solite Gasoline
double-sided porcelain sign, with Ethyl logo, fair condition, faded and numerous dime-size chips in field, 30" diameter.

$250+

Speedwell Oil
single-sided tin sign, very good condition, 7 1/2" by 20 1/2".

$25+

Stanocola Gasoline Polarine
We Sell Nothing But Stancola Products single-sided porcelain, good condition, four dime-size chips in field and minor wear, 14" by 24".

$550+

Stanocola Gasoline
porcelain flange sign, very good condition, one touchup, 20" by 22".

$1,000+

Stanocola Polarine
porcelain flange sign, very good condition, edge chips on reverse, 20" by 22".

$1,000+

Stanocola Polarine
single-sided porcelain sign, fair condition, edge chips, porcelain worn at bottom, 18" by 36", rare.

$250+

Stanocola
Standard Oil Company of Louisiana double-sided porcelain sign, good condition, several areas professionally touched up, 30" diameter.

$3,000+

Stanocola
Standard Oil of Louisiana single-sided porcelain sign, excellent condition, small edge chips and one chip in outer ring, 18" diameter.

$5,000+

Standard Automotive Diesel Fuel
double-sided porcelain sign, near mint, 12" diameter.

$450+

Standard Burner Oils Dealer
single-sided porcelain die-cut sign, very good condition, quarter-size chip at bottom mounting hole, minor chips around edge, 30" by 48".

$700+

Standard Burner Oils Dealer
single-sided porcelain sign, very good condition, 2" chip on edge, small chip in field, 30" by 48".

$700+

Standard Burner Oils
die-cut single-sided porcelain, good condition, 7 1/2" by 14".

$350+

Standard Burner Oils
die-cut single-sided porcelain sign, excellent condition-plus, 9" by 14".

$625+

Standard Credit Cards Honored
double-sided porcelain sign, good condition with chips around mounting holes, 12" by 18".

$300+

Standard
embossed pricer, good condition, 7" by 10".

$425+

Standard Ethyl
for Winter Driving cardboard winter-front, good condition, with dust staining.

$500+

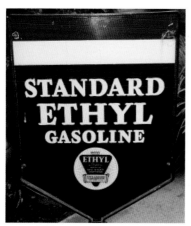

Standard Ethyl Gasoline
hallmark double-sided porcelain sign, very good condition, small chips, original base, 27" by 21" without base.

$1,200+

Standard Ethyl Gasoline
single-sided porcelain with early Ethyl logo, excellent condition, made for display with 42" Red Crown Zerolene sign, 33" by 21".

$850+

Standard Gasoline
1940 Walt Disney Mickey Mouse sign, very good condition, light wear, 24" diameter.

$4,750+

Standard Gasoline
and Motor Oils double-sided porcelain sign, fair condition, low gloss, chips at mounting holes, 30" diameter.

$300+

Standard Gasoline
single-sided porcelain sign, fair to good condition, chips around mounting holes, 18" by 36".

$175+

Standard Gasoline Unsurpassed
winter-front, near mint, framed, 13" by 17".

$100+

Standard Gasoline Unsurpassed
winter-front, very good condition, small blemish at top, framed, 11" by 15".

$125+

Standard Gasoline Unsurpassed
winter-front, excellent condition, blemish in center of field, dated 1926, framed, 13" by 17".

$100+

Standard Heating Oil Delivery Truck
single-sided tin sign, fair condition, wear and scratches in field, 21" by 44".

$600+

Standard Heating Oils
single-sided porcelain sign with hallmark, near mint, 20" by 16".

$625+

Standard Heating Oils
single-sided porcelain with hallmark, blue border ring, near mint, 13" by 10".

$875+

Standard Heating Oils
single-sided porcelain die-cut sign, fair to good condition, chips around mounting holes, minor wear in field, 18" by 28".

$350+

Standard Heating Oils
single-sided porcelain die-cut sign, very good condition, scratches in field, quarter-size chip lower left, dime-size chip upper right, 30" by 40".

$500+

Standard Heating Oils
single-sided porcelain with hallmark, near mint, 13" by 10".

$200+

Standard
Koolmotor and De Luxe cardboard winter-fronts, fair condition or less.

$60+ all

Standard Motor Gasoline
porcelain flange, display side fair to good condition, large chip and crazing, reverse fair, 24" by 24".

$400+

Standard Motor Gasoline Service Station
porcelain flange sign, Stancola, excellent condition, one chip on both sides, 18" by 24".

$500+

Standard Oil Calol-Zerolene
porcelain flange sign, display side good condition with light wear and repaired bullet hole, reverse fair with more wear and chipping, 24" by 17".

$2,900+

Standard Motor Oil
single-sided porcelain sign, very good condition, some edge chipping, 18" by 36".

$800+

Standard Gasoline
1939 Walt Disney Mickey Mouse winter-front, very good condition, minor fading, framed, 13" by 16".

$1,600+

Standard Oil Company
of California Red Crown single-sided porcelain truck sign, good condition, chips at mounting holes, 10" diameter.

$1,200+

Standard Oil Company
meter single-sided tin sign, very good condition, edge chips, 5" by 8".

$400+

Standard Motor Oil
single-sided porcelain dome sign, excellent condition, chipped upper right, 8" by 11 1/2".

$550+

Standard Oil Company
Positively No Smoking embossed single-sided tin, very good condition, light staining, 6" by 11".

$225+

Standard Oil Company Reward
single-sided porcelain sign, very good condition, minor chipping at mounting holes, 8" by 11".

$300+

Standard Oil Company
single-sided porcelain truck cab sign, very good condition, edge chipping, 9" by 14".

$300+

Standard Oil
Credit Cards Good Here die-cut tin flange, display side very good condition with minor paint loss, reverse fair to good with flaking, 26" by 24".

$400+

Standard Oil
of Indiana Safety First single-sided tin sign, good condition, 8" by 10".

$300+

Standard Oil
of Indiana Safety First single-sided porcelain sign, very good condition, chipped lower left corner, 18" by 12".

$450+

Standard Oil
New Jersey single-sided porcelain, very good condition, minor edge chipping, small chip in field, 10" square.

$725+

Standard Oil
of New Jersey single-sided flange, very good condition, 9" by 12 1/2".

$125+

Standard Oil
of New Jersey No Smoking single-sided porcelain sign, very good condition, dime-size chip at center mounting hole, edge chip, 4 1/2" by 24".

$375+

Standard Oil Stanavo
single-sided porcelain sign, excellent condition, chips around mounting holes, 5 1/2" by 20".

$750+

Standard Oil Products
"cloud" double-sided porcelain sign, neon added, very good to excellent condition, three chips in field, 30" by 60".

$2,600+

Standard Oil
of New Jersey Wholesale Only single-sided porcelain truck sign, near mint, 13" by 10".

$600+

Standard Oil Safety First
single-sided tin sign, dated 1930, good condition, 14" by 10".

$25+

Standard Oil
(Texas) Products double-sided porcelain sign, excellent condition, scratches in field, 33" diameter.

$375+

Standard Oil
of Texas Products double-sided porcelain sign, excellent condition, chip on edge, 33" diameter.

$900+

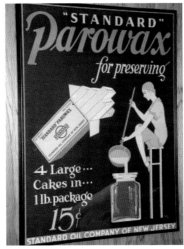

Standard Parowax
poster, near mint, framed, 24" by 18".

$200+

Standard Products
"cloud" single-sided porcelain sign, excellent condition-plus, 24" diameter.

$1,900+

Standard RPM Lubrication
porcelain flange, near mint, 19" by 22".

$1,950+

Standard Safety Check Lubrication
single-sided porcelain sign, excellent condition, chip at mounting hole, 4" diameter.

$130+

Standard
single-sided tin sign with hallmark, very good condition, some wear, 42" diameter.

$200+

Standard Oil Warning
single-sided porcelain sign, excellent condition, minor edge chips, 4" by 9".
$200+

Standard Of Texas
No Smoking single-sided porcelain sign, excellent condition, 12" by 30".
$600+

Standard Service
No Tipping Please (Stanocola) single-sided porcelain sign, excellent condition, large chip touched up in upper left corner, 12" by 16".
$275+

Standard Station Inc.
Authorized Distributor single-sided porcelain sign, fair to good condition, several touchups, 60" by 33".
$100+

Sunoco Restrooms
double-sided porcelain hanging sign, excellent condition, chips around mounting holes, 6 1/2" by 21".
$700+

Sunoco
cardboard winter-fronts, one fair to good condition, one poor.
$120+ pair

Sunoco
(Blue) 200 single-sided porcelain die-cut pump plate, excellent condition-plus, 21" by 15".
$300+

Sunoco
(French) Men restroom single-sided porcelain die-cut sign, near mint, 4" by 9".

$350+

Sunoco Men and Ladies
restroom single-sided porcelain signs, near mint, each 3" by 7".

$800+ pair

Sunray
Danger No Smoking single-sided porcelain sign, excellent condition, 10" by 14".

$550+

Super Greyhound Motor Fuel
double-sided porcelain, very good to excellent condition, two quarter-size chips upper left, minor chipping around edge, 34" by 58".

$2,600+

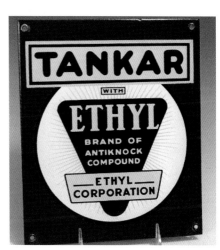

Sunset New Ethyl
single-sided cardboard sign, 27" by 43".

$125+

Tankar Regular
porcelain pump plate, excellent condition, 8 1/2" by 10".

No established value

Tankar Ethyl
porcelain pump plate, near mint condition, 8 1/2" by 10".

No established value

Texaco Aviation Fuels
& Lubricants single-sided tin sign, fair condition, 30" by 48".

$1,900+

Texaco
(black T) Gasoline Filling Station single-sided
porcelain sign, good condition, small chips in field
and around mounting holes, 42" diameter.

$2,750+

Texaco Battery Service
single-sided porcelain sign, good condition, has chips around mounting holes,
8" by 22 1/2".

$375+

Texaco
(black T) Gasoline-Motor Oil double-sided
porcelain sign, very good to excellent condition,
two chips in field and chipping around mounting
holes, 42" diameter.

$1,250+

Texaco
(black T) "keyhole" single-sided porcelain truck
sign, near mint.

$475+

Texaco
(black T) Motor Oil Clean, Clear Golden porcelain flange sign, fair to good condition, has been
touched up on both sides, 23" by 18".

$350+

Texaco
(black T) double-sided porcelain sign, fair condition with chips and holes rusted through, 42"
diameter.

$550+

Texaco
(black T) double-sided porcelain station canopy
sign with base, dated 1938, excellent to near mint,
15" tall.

$2,100+

Texaco
(black T) single-sided porcelain keyhole sign, dated 1935, very good condition, chips around edge, 15 1/2" by 10 1/2".

$500+

Texaco
(black T) single-sided porcelain lubster sign, near mint.

$325+

Texaco
(black T) single-sided porcelain pump plate, dated 1930, excellent condition, 15" diameter.

$350+

Texaco
double-sided porcelain identification sign, dated 1955, good condition, 72" diameter.

$275+

Texaco Diesel Chief
(diesel fuel) single-sided porcelain pump plate, dated 1956, very good condition, chips around two mounting holes, 18" by 12".

$175+

Texaco Diesel Chief "L"
(diesel fuel) single-sided porcelain pump plate, dated 1962, excellent condition, 18" by 12".

$325+

Texaco Diesel Chief
single-sided tin embossed pump plate, near mint, 10" by 15".

$275+

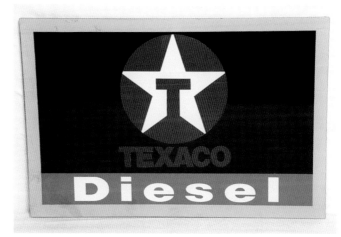

Texaco Diesel
single-sided tin reflective sign, excellent condition-plus, 12" by 18".

$90+

Texaco Fire Chief Gasoline
porcelain pump plate, dated 1940, near mint, 12"
by 8".

$500+

Texaco Fire Chief Gasoline
porcelain pump plate, dated 1942, excellent condition, 12" by 8".

$175+

Texaco Fire Chief Gasoline
porcelain pump plate, dated 1943, excellent condition, 18" by 12".

$125+

Texaco Fire Chief
porcelain pump plate, dated 1961, very good
condition, damage on top left mounting hole, 18"
by 12".

$80+

Texaco Fire Chief
porcelain pump plate, dated 1963, good condition,
18" by 12".

$100+

Texaco Fire Chief Gasoline
single-sided porcelain pump plate, dated 1963,
very good condition, some rust, 18" by 12".

$100+

Texaco Fire Chief
single-sided porcelain pump plate, dated 1965,
good condition, 18" by 12".

$80+

Texaco Fire Chief Gasoline
porcelain pump plate, good condition, small chips
around edge, 12" by 8".

$150+

Texaco Fire Chief
single-sided porcelain curved pump plate, dated
1940, good condition, chips around edge and
mounting holes, 18" by 10".

$100+

Texaco Fire Chief
single-sided porcelain pump plate, dated 1951, good condition, chips around edge and mounting holes, 18" by 12".

$110+

Texaco Marine White Gasoline
porcelain pump plate, 1960, excellent condition, small ships around mounting holes.

$900+

Texaco
porcelain pump plate, fair to good condition, significant edge chipping, 8" diameter.

$75+

Texaco Marfak Lubrication
single-sided tin sign, good condition, 24" by 40".

$200+

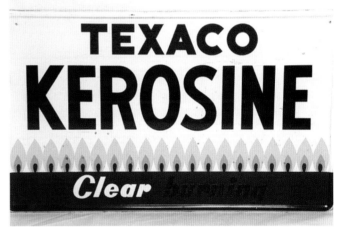

Texaco Kerosine
single-sided tin sign, excellent condition-plus, 12" by 20".

$200+

Texaco Marine Products
single-sided porcelain sign, poor to fair condition, 25 1/2" by 96".

$650+

Texaco No Smoking
single-sided porcelain sign with black border, dated 1946, good condition, 4" by 23".

$150+

Texaco Fire Chief
wood sign, fair to good condition, weathered, 12" by 30".

$50+

Texaco Motor Oil Insulated
double-sided porcelain sign, excellent condition, with small touched-up chip, 11" by 14".

$425+

Texaco No Smoking
single-sided porcelain sign, fair condition, 4" by 23".

$150+

Texaco No Smoking
single-sided porcelain sign, restored, 6" by 24".

$2,000+

Texaco
porcelain letters mounted truck topper, excellent condition, 6" by 48".

$750+

Texaco Motor Oil Insulated
double-sided tin sign, dated 1952, excellent condition, 11" by 21 1/2".

$175+

Texaco Motor Oil Insulated
double-sided tin sign, dated 1948, near mint, 11" by 21".

$250+

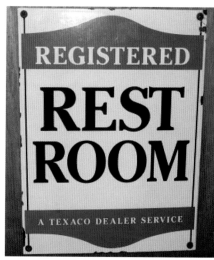

Texaco Rest Room
single-sided porcelain sign, very good condition, edge chipping, 12" by 9".

$300+

Texaco
single-sided tin sign, 19 1/2" by 13 1/2".

$550

Texaco
single-sided porcelain pump plate, dated 1946, good condition, small chips in field, 15" diameter.

$150+

Texaco Sky Chief Gasoline
porcelain pump plate, dated 1946, near mint, 12" by 8".

$500+

Texaco Sky Chief Petrox
single-sided porcelain pump plate, dated 1955, very good condition, chips around mounting holes, 22" by 12".

$100+

Texaco Sky Chief
porcelain pump plate, good condition, has chips along edges, 18" by 12".

$50+

Texaco Sky Chief Su-preme
porcelain pump plate, excellent condition-plus, small chips along bottom edge, 12" by 8".

$200+

Texaco Sky Chief Su-preme
porcelain pump plate, dated 1963, good condition, small chips and some rust along edge, 18" by 20".

$50+

Texaco Sky Chief Su-preme
single-sided porcelain pump plate, dated 1959, very good condition, 18" by 12".

$150+

Texaco Sky Chief Su-preme
single-sided porcelain pump plate, dated 1962, good condition, 18" by 12".

$100+

Texaco Sky Chief Su-preme
single-sided porcelain pump plate, dated 1965, excellent condition, some chips, 18" by 12".

$80+

Tide Water Associated
Certified Clean Comfort Stations single-sided tin sign, excellent condition with a few scratches, 30" diameter.

Texaco
and Union cardboard winter-fronts, poor to good condition.

$110+ all

$600+

Tide Water Oil Products Distributor
single-sided porcelain sign, good condition, some staining and scratches, 7" by 16".

$175+

Tide Water Associated
single-sided porcelain truck sign, near mint, 7 1/2" by 11".

$825+

Time Premium Gasoline
porcelain pump plate, new old stock, 14" by 9 1/2".

$950+

Time Super Gasoline
porcelain pump plate, very good condition, small chip in upper left corner, 14" by 9".

$950+

Triton
one Deluxe and one Amoco cardboard winter-fronts, fair condition or less.

$40+ all

Tydol
cardboard winter-fronts, two good condition, one fair.

$150+ all

Tydol
and two Flying A cardboard winter-fronts, each good condition.

$75+ all

Ultra-Power
single-sided porcelain embossed sign, excellent condition-plus, 8" by 13".

$100+

Union 76 Gasoline
porcelain pump plate, near mint, 13" diameter.

$150+

Union 76
Authorized Automatic Transmission Service single-sided porcelain sign, excellent condition-plus, 12" diameter.

$275+

Union 76 Gasoline
porcelain pump plate, very good condition, chip on one mounting hole, 11 1/2" diameter.

$125+

Union 76 Outboard Fuel Gasoline
porcelain pump plate, good condition, chip on left mounting hole, 11 1/2" diameter.
$150+

Union 76 Outboard Fuel Pre-Mix
double-sided porcelain sign, excellent condition, small chips, 42" diameter.
$850+

Union 76 Regular Gasoline
porcelain pump plate, excellent condition, 18" by 14".
$225+

Union 76 Private Property
single-sided porcelain sign, very good condition, small chip and wear throughout field, 12" by 24".
$150+

Union 76 Royal Gasoline
single-sided porcelain pump plate, very good condition, staining around edge, 11 1/2" diameter.
$100+

Union 76 Royal Marine Gasoline
single-sided porcelain pump plate, good condition with chips around sides, 11 1/2" diameter.
$325+

Union 76
single-sided porcelain die-cut truck door sign, excellent condition, minor edge chip, 7" by 7".
$2,900+

Union 76
single-sided porcelain truck sign, excellent condition-plus, 8" diameter.
$450+

Union 76
single-sided porcelain pump plates, each 18" by 14", one fair condition, one good.

$200+ pair

Union 76
Stop Your Motor/No Smoking single-sided porcelain sign, good condition, chips around mounting holes, 6" by 30".

$225+

Union 76 No Smoking
double-sided porcelain sign, excellent condition, minor chipping at mounting holes, 6" by 30".

$500+

Union 76 Triton Motor Oil
single-sided porcelain sign, excellent condition, small chips around one mounting hole, 12" by 14".

$250+

Union No Trespassing
single-sided porcelain sign, near mint, 8" by 24".

$550+

Union Products No Smoking
double-sided porcelain sign, excellent condition, 6" by 30".

$2,000+

Union 76
Underground Cable single-sided porcelain sign, fair to good condition, damage around mounting holes, 14" by 10".

$40+

Union 76 Unifuel
Marine Diesel Fuel, pump plate, excellent condition, very small chip on top edge, 11 1/2" diameter.

$275+

Union 76
neon single-sided porcelain sign, poor to fair condition, touched up, 52" by 41".

$650+

Union 76 Unifuel
porcelain pump plate, excellent condition, 11 1/2" diameter.

$150+

Union 7600 Gasoline
porcelain pump plate, excellent condition, small scratch in field, 11 1/2" diameter.

$150+

Union Diesol Diesel Fuel
pump plate, good condition, large chip on top mounting hole, 12" diameter.

$150+

Union Gasoline
double-sided porcelain sign, display side fair to good condition, reverse poor to fair, 42" diameter.

$450+

Union Gasoline Speed & Power
die-cut double-sided porcelain sign, display side very good condition with small chips in field, reverse good with larger chips, 32" by 26".

$1,200+

Union Oil Minute Man Service
double-sided porcelain sign, excellent condition, chips around top mounting holes.

$7,000+

Union Products
single-sided porcelain sign, good condition, may be part of another sign, 6" diameter.

$200+

Union Women's Room
porcelain flange, excellent condition, 12" by 10".

$250+

Union Women's Room
single-sided porcelain sign, excellent condition, 13" by 12".

$300+

United Motors Service
(with arrow, rare) double-sided porcelain sign, new old stock, 42" by 18".

$6,000+

Vacuum Motor Car Oils
(Mobiloil) porcelain flange, display side fair condition, reverse poor with edge chips and fading, 16" by 20".

$100+

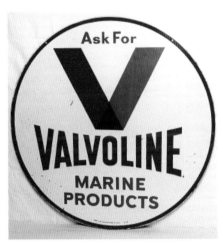

Valvoline Motor Oil
double-sided tin sign, fair to good condition, 32" by 48".

$325+

Valvoline Marine Products
double-sided tin sign, fair condition, 30" diameter.

$75+

Veedol Chain Oil
single-sided tin sign, very good condition, 12" by 32".

$275+

Veltex Fletcher Oil Company
truck door single-sided porcelain sign, excellent condition, small chip at mounting hole, 16" diameter.

$2,500+

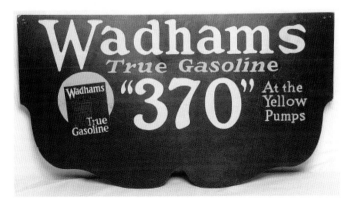

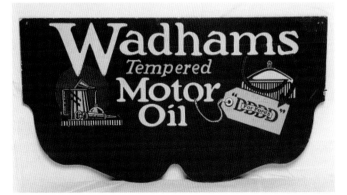

Wadhams "370" True Gasoline
die-cut cardboard winter-front, excellent condition.

$275+

Wadhams Tempered Motor Oil
die-cut cardboard winter-front, very good condition.

$300+

White Rose
double-sided porcelain sign, near mint, 18" by 17 1/2".

$200+

White Rose
single-sided porcelain sign, fair condition with chips and wear, 36" diameter.

$700+

Wil-Flo Motor Oil
double-sided tin oval sign, 17" by 23", display side restored, reverse total loss.

$3,100+

Winthrop Oil Co.
embossed pointer single-sided tin sign, poor to fair condition, stained, 6 1/2" by 27".

$175+

Wolf's Head Motor Oil
tin flange sign, dated 1964, excellent condition.

$250+

Zerolene "F" for Fords
poster, excellent condition, framed, 29" by 21".

$800+

Zerolene For Correct Lubrication
single-sided porcelain sign, very good condition, quarter-size chips at mounting holes, 15" by 20".

$700+

Zerolene Standard Oil
for Motor Boats porcelain flange, display side good condition with crazing and wear, reverse fair to good with crazing, 24" by 24".

$1,600+

Zerolene Standard Oil
for Motor Cars porcelain flange, display side very good condition with slight wear and crazing, reverse fair to good with wear and crazing, slight warp, clear coated, 24" by 24".

$1,600+

Zerolene Standard Oil
of California single-sided porcelain truck sign, poor condition, 10" diameter.

$325+

Zerolene Motor Oil
Solvent Refined double-sided tin sign, excellent
condition, paper mark, 11" square.

$225+

Zerolene Oils and Grease
for Correct Lubrication SSY self-framed sign,
excellent condition, 19" by 54".

$450+

Zerolene
single-sided tin sign, good condition with wear
and scrapes in field, framed, 18" by 53".

$300+

Zerolene
(Spanish) porcelain flange, very good condition,
minor edge chips, some fading, 14" by 15".

$1,000+

Zerolene
(The New) "lollipop" double-sided porcelain sign,
very good to excellent condition, chips at mounting
holes, glossy, original base, 27" by 27", not including base.

$900+

Zerolene
The Standard Oil for Motor Cars single-sided
porcelain sign, near-mint-plus, 8" diameter.

$3,100+

Zerolene
The Standard Oil for Motor Cars single-sided
porcelain sign, fair condition, chips around edge
and mounting holes, 6" diameter.

$700+

Zerolene
The Standard Oil for Motor Cars single-sided porcelain sign,
good condition, three touched-up chips around edge, 24"
diameter.

$1,900+

Zerolene
The Standard Oil for Motor Cars single-sided porcelain tank wagon sign, poor
to fair condition, large chips around mounting holes, 9" by 24".

$225+

Other Petroliana Items

This section offers a diverse petroliana group that includes ashtrays, awards, attendants' caps, banks, dolls, clocks, clothing, dinnerware, figurines, first-aid kits, lamps, license plate tags, lights, lighters, maps, paperweights, penholders, pin-back buttons, thermometers, toys, trophies, even salt and pepper shakers.

Amoco
horseshoe-shape tin license plate tag, excellent condition.
$110+

Atlantic White Flash
and Fleet Wing license plate tags, good condition and poor to fair.
$100+ pair

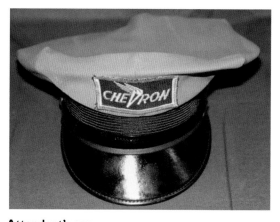

Attendant's cap
with Chevron patch, good condition.
$50+

Attendant's cap
with Chevron patch, good condition.
$25+

Attendant's cap
with Chevron patch, good condition.
$40+

Attendant's cap
with SCO embroidered patch, good condition.

$80+

Attendant's cap
with Standard celluloid pin-back button, good condition.

$125+

Attendant's cap
with Standard Hallmark porcelain badge, good condition.

$60+

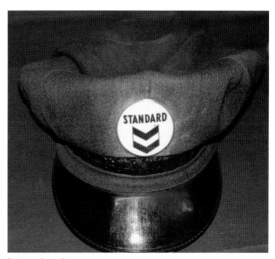

Attendant's cap
with Standard Hallmark porcelain badge, good condition.

$70+

Banks
(glass): Tankar System Save, Esso, Sohio.

$10+ each

Banks
(tin): Allstate, two different, excellent condition.

$30+ pair

Buddy Lee doll
in Chevron uniform, plastic body, excellent condition.

$750+

Buddy Lee Standard Oil doll
with stand, plastic body, good condition, 14" tall.

$375+

Buddy Lee Standard Oil doll
with stand, plastic body, good condition, 14" tall.

$300+

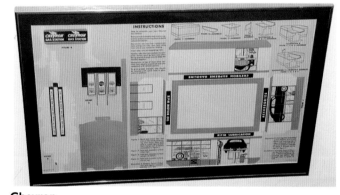

Chevron
punch-out gas station set, 1947, excellent condition, 16" by 24".

$100+

Calso Gasoline clock
good condition, paint loss on two numbers, 14" diameter.

$425+

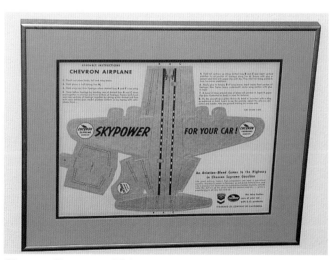

Chevron Skypower Glider
excellent condition, framed, 13" by 16".

$25+

Chevron Supreme
and Chevron Dealer lighters.

$40+ pair

Chevron Gas Pump
salt and pepper shaker, good condition.

$140+ pair

Chevron Shipping Co.
Lucite paperweight, 6" by 5", excellent condition.

$25+

Chevron
tank truck and plant snow dome paperweight,
near mint, 4" tall.

$125+

Chevron
die-cast tiger pull toy, "I Got Live Power," minor wear, 4" by 4 1/2".

$300+

En-Ar-Co boy
with chalkboard license plate tag, good condition.

$130+

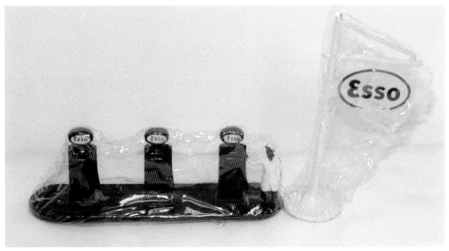

Esso Matchbox
gas pump island and sign, in original plastic wrap.

$30+ set

Fil-A-Lite
(visible pump style), near mint, 17" tall.

$1,900+

Fleet-Wing Tin
license plate tag, very good condition.

$150+

Fleet-Wing
license plate tag, excellent condition.

$130+

Flying A Giant Power
die-cut tin license plate tag, good condition.

$210+

Gas station
island light.

$900+

Hancock Lighter
excellent condition.

$50+

Jenney Aero
Gasoline tip tray.

$175+

Johnson Brilliant Bronze
Drive Safely license plate tag with reflector, excellent condition.

$40+

Johnson
Motor Oil bank.

$125+

Koolmotor Bronze Gasoline
celluloid pin-back button, excellent condition.

$50+

Lion Naturalube
license plate tag, fair to good condition.

$120+

Marathon Running Man
Best in Long Run tin license plate tag, very good condition, some wear.

$100+

Mobil
10-year service ashtray, good condition.

$325+

Mobil
10-year service ashtray, good condition.

$225+

Mobil
20-year service award bookends, good condition.

$425+ pair

Mobil
paperweight, good condition.

$425+

Mobil
15-year service penholder.

$225+

Mobil
desk penholder.

$200+

Five Mobil
service awards, all with some damage.

$500+ all

Mobil
coin-operated riding horse, this is one of five that were made for display
at Mobil stations, restored condition, original chaps, 64" by 55" by 70".

$28,000+

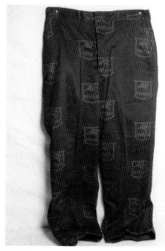

Mobilgas
trousers.

$100+

Mobilgas
wind-up toy service station by Cragstan, very good condition, missing original key.

$40+

Mobil Pegasus
Refill with Mobilheat coal bucket.

$100+

Mobil Pegasus
America First die-cut embossed tin license plate tag, poor to fair condition.

$80+

Mobil Pegasus
California World's Fair die-cut tin license plate tag, excellent condition, minor wear.

$200+

Mobil Pegasus
California World's Fair tin license plate tag, very good condition.

$150+

Two Mobil Pegasus
license plate tags, fair condition.

$100+ pair

Two Mobil Pegasus
license plate tags, fair condition and very poor.

$80+ pair

Mobil Shield
eight 9 1/2" plates.

$50+ all

Mobil Socony
1945 calendar, near mint, framed, 29" by 25".

$25+

Mohawk Gasoline
celluloid pin-back button, 2 1/4" diameter, excellent condition.

$300+

Paperweights
four dome-top glass for Polarine, Red Crown, Standard Ethyl and ISO-VIS, all good condition.

$400+ all

Pennsylvania Producer
tin license plate tag, excellent condition, light rust.

$70+

Pennzoil
celluloid pin-back button, with owl, "Member Oil-Wise Club," excellent condition.

$35+

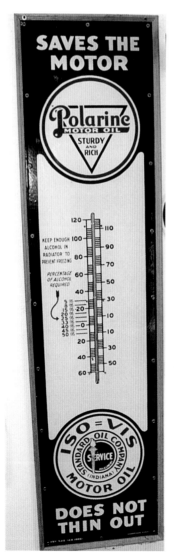

Phillips 66
Safety Pays die-cut tin license plate tag, light scratches.

$150+

Polarine ISO-VIS
single-sided porcelain thermometer, excellent condition, small chip below Polarine logo, 72" by 18".

$3,000+

Pure Drive Safely
license plate tags, fair to good condition.

$110+ pair

Red Crown Gasoline
Polarine Motor Oil single-sided porcelain thermometer, good condition, quarter-size chips around mounting holes, dime-size chip in field, missing glass, original wood frame in fair condition, 72" by 18".

$1,500+

Red Crown Gasoline
Polarine for Power Mileage Made in Four Grades single-sided porcelain thermometer, good condition, glass missing, minor chipping top and bottom, quarter-size chip in field, original wood frame fair condition, 72" by 18".

$2,000+

Red Crown Gasoline
for Power Mileage single-sided porcelain thermometer, fair condition, large chip middle left edge.

$1,400+

Richfield
bronze plaque service award, good condition, 12" by 8 1/2".

$175+

Shell
Buddy L. dump truck, missing grille.

$70+

Shell
(Gold) tin license plate tag, excellent condition.

$20+

Shell
Sunoco and D-X license plate tags, fair condition or less.

$70+ all

Shell
embossed tin clam license plate tags, both good condition.

$40+ pair

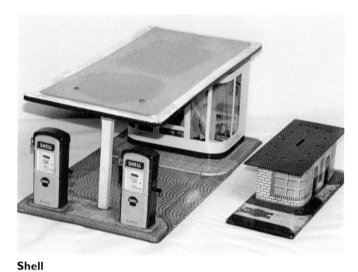

Shell
tin litho service station and bank.

$140+ pair

Signal 10-30 HD Motor Oil
tin coin bank, excellent condition.

$75+

Sinclair Oilers
baseball uniform, with shirt, pants and socks.

$100+ set

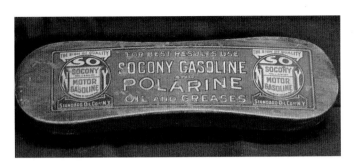

Socony Gasoline
upholstery brush, 2" by 7", very good condition.

$50+

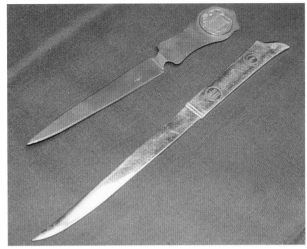

Socony
and Calso-RPM letter openers.

$25+ pair

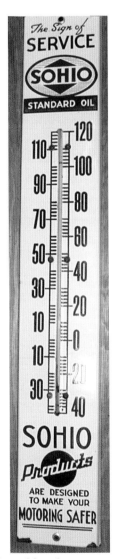

Sohio Sign of Service
porcelain thermometer, excellent condition, chips at corners, 34" by 5".

$1,400+

Socony Polarine Products
Celluloid Pocket Mirror, very good condition, mirror worn at edges, 3 1/2" diameter.

$50+

Sohio Petroleum Products
enamel hat badge, good condition.

$125+

Standard Oil
Employee porcelain car badge, near mint, 3" wide.

$1,900+

Standard Gasoline
"Unsurpassed" celluloid pin-back button, excellent condition.

$50+

Standard
and Chevron lighters.

$45+ pair

Standard Heating Oils
and RPM Motor Oils lighters, in original boxes, good condition.

$90+ pair

Standard Oil
highway maps, one dated 1924.

$80+ pair

Standard Oil
Olympic Year road maps, one dated 1929, one 1932.

$100+ pair

Standard Wild to Go
Cowboy decal, excellent condition, 5" by 5", matted.

$15+

Standard Wild to Go
Santa paper item, good condition.

$20+

Standard Oil
of California brass flag pole emblem, excellent condition, 7" by 6".

$550+

Standard Oil
of California cylinder first-aid kit, with contents, good condition, 12" long.

$150+

Standard Oil
of California 1936 "NODOME" lead figurine, excellent condition, minor paint loss, 5 1/4" tall.

$40+

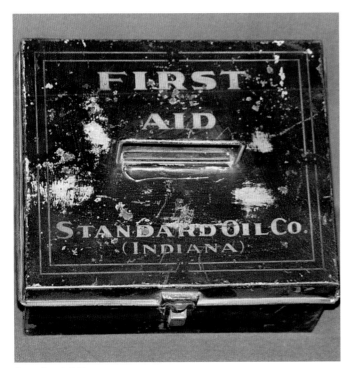

Standard Oil
of Indiana first-aid kit, with contents, fair condition.

$150+

Standard Oil Company
of California training game, excellent condition, minor stain, dated 1960.

$60+

Standard Oil Company
of California 1926 Wild To Go paper pennant.

$15+

Standard Oil Company
of Indiana porcelain paperweight, worn, 3 1/4"
diameter.

$75+

Standard Oil
of Indiana wall sconce, rust pitting, repainted, with original Red
Crown globe in good condition, 15" by 14".

$625+

Standard Oil
with crowns salt and pepper shaker, good condition.

$190+ pair

Standard Oil
of Kentucky map of Georgia, 1925, framed, 13" by 16".

$300+

Standard Oil Polarine
for Motor Boats & Motor Cars pocket mirror, 2"
diameter.

$75+

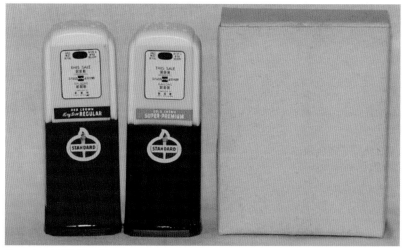

Standard Oil Gas Pump
salt and pepper shaker with box, good condition.

$80+ pair

Standard
of Kentucky lighter, NIB.

$75+

Standard Oil Red Crown
Gas Pump salt and pepper shaker, good condition.

$110+ pair

Standard Red Crown
paper pop gun, 1938, excellent condition.

$25+

Standard Oil
Save with Standard Buy War Savings Bonds glass block bank, 4 1/2" square.

$100+

Standard Oil
Watch Your Savings Grow with Standard Oil Products glass block bank, 4 1/2" square.

$50+

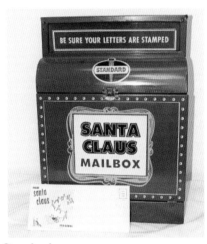

Standard
Santa Claus Mailbox, with letter, excellent condition, 17 1/2" by 12 1/2".

$275+

Standard Products
Swede's Garage tin license plate tag, excellent condition.

$30+

Standard Red Crown
Research Test Car die-cut tin license plate tag, minor wear.

$175+

Standard Station
first-aid kit.

$15+

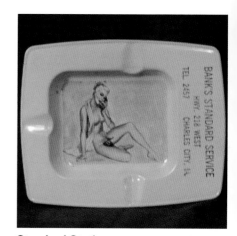

Standard Oil Station
first-aid kit, with contents.

$15+

Standard Station
tin ashtray with nude woman, near mint.

$100+

Sunset Oil Company
thermometer, good condition.

$350+

Texaco Burn Roundup Coal
license plate tag, very good condition, rust along bottom.

$175+

Texaco
tanker trucks by Brown and Bigelow and AMF.

$70+ all

Texaco
tanker truck by Buddy L.

$100+

Texaco
tanker truck by Buddy L., and Texaco fire engine by AMF with damage.

$120+ pair

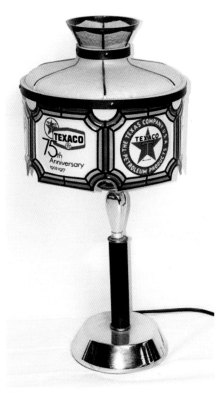

Texaco
75th anniversary plastic desk lamp, excellent condition.

$125+

Standard tanker trucks

$80+ all

Tootsie Toy
Standard tankers, in "played with" condition.

$60+ pair

Tydol Yellow Man
with oil can license plate tag, near mint.

$200+

Tydol
plastic racer car with original balloon, good condition.

$80+

Tydol
(broken) and Veedol die-cut embossed tin license plate tags, fair condition and very poor.

$130+ pair

Veedol Red Man
with oil can license plate tag, good condition, overall wear.

$80+

White Crown
Standard swag lamp, no hardware, very good condition.

$225+

White Rose En-Ar-Co Boy
with slate die-cut tin license plate tag, excellent condition, wear around edges.

$100+

Woco Pep Drive Safely
license plate tag, good condition, minor wear.

$100+

Zerolene
trophy, made by Heinz Art Metal, excellent condition.

$250+

Related Items

"Related" collectibles—often automotive in nature—that appeal to petroliana collectors, but are not directly tied to the production of oil and gasoline, include things like tires, spark plugs, heaters, etc., and transportation in general. An emerging subcategory featured here includes advertising for bus lines and depots.

1939 Golden Gate
International Exposition tin license plate tag, good condition, faded.

$100+

Acadian Lines
Bus Stop Sign porcelain flange, excellent condition, metal loss on flange, 24" by 19".

$1,600+

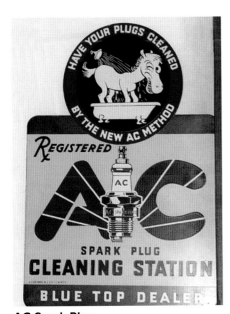

AC Spark Plug
metal flange sign, dated 1936, near mint, 15" by 10 1/2".

$650+

AC Spark Plug
tin thermometer with horse, good condition, some wear and staining, 21" by 7".

$200+

American Brakeblok
tin thermometer, dated 1958, excellent condition, 20" by 6".

$80+

American Flag
die-cut tin license plate tag, near mint.

$70+

Atlas Tires
clock, good condition, needs work on motor, 19" diameter.

$325+

Atlas Tires
clock, dome face, does not run, 17" diameter.

$300+

Atlas Tires Batteries Accessories
octagon clock with neon, excellent condition, pin-head paint loss in blue border, 18" by 18".

$1,050+

Atlas Tires
vertical single-sided porcelain self-framed sign, with Standard Oil logo, good condition, two silver-dollar-size chips in field, 60" by 16".

$225+

Auto Club of America
L.A. Cal. Official die-cut flange sign, excellent condition to near mint, 10" by 10".

$1,700+

Auto Lite Spark Plugs
display case, good condition, 18" by 13".

$50+

Auto-Lite Official Service
die-cut porcelain flange, excellent condition-plus, 13 1/2" by 14".

$2,000+

Automobile Club
of Southern California embossed tin license plate tag.

$50+

Beacon Wax Authorized Dealer
reverse-painted backlit counter display, excellent condition, 11 1/2" square.

$350+

Bear
neon and porcelain sign, neon replaced and minor touchups, 64" tall.

$3,000

Betty Radiator Mascot
decal with original packaging, 4" by 10" framed, very good condition.

$100+

Blaupunkt Autoradio
figural die-cut single-sided tin sign, near mint, 16" by 9".

$475+

Bluebird Coach Lines Bus Depot
porcelain flange, restored, 14" by 20".

$1,400+

Buick Lubricare
neon sign, all original, 13 feet long. (Collector Tip: This is the larger version of the sign; the smaller version is harder to find and worth about $3,300+.)

$2,800+

Buick
Authorized Buick Service double sided porcelain sign, original hangers, 42" diameter, near mint.

$3,500+

Burd Hi-Speed Piston Rings
double-sided tin die-cut hanging sign, near mint, 11 1/2" by 18".

$4,000+

Burlington Trailways American Buslines
backlit counter display, excellent condition, hairline cracks in plastic, 9 1/2" by 11".

$450+

Burlington National Trailways System
Bus Depot double-sided porcelain sign, excellent condition-plus, minor scratches, 22" square.

$800+

Burlington Route Bus Depot
double-sided porcelain sign, near mint, 9 1/2" by 23".

$1,300+

Bus line guides
one Gray Line, one Pickwick Greyhound Lines.

$35+ pair

Buss Auto Fuses
metal counter-top display rack, excellent condition, 7 1/2" by 8 1/2" by 3".

$450+

Calumet Chief Colorado Coal
die-cut single-sided porcelain sign, excellent condition, chip in corner, 18" by 16".

$2,000+

Carlisle Tires Keep Cool
porcelain flange, dated 1921, display side excellent condition with small chips, reverse very good with quarter-size chip on right edge, 19" by 26".

$700+

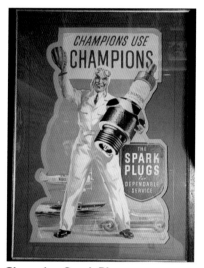

Carter Carburetor Gasket
tin rack, excellent condition, full, 42" by 17".

$400+

Champion Spark Plug
cardboard display, excellent condition, light wear, framed and matted, 32" by 22".

$2,100+

Champion
AM/FM radio, working condition.

$50+

Champion
service kit tin box, good condition.

$20+

Champion
We Clean and Check Spark Plugs single-sided tin sign, new old stock (?), 14" by 30".

$350+

Champion Dealer Service
tin flange, near mint, 12" by 16".

$675+

Champion Double Ribbed Spark Plugs
single-sided tin sign, new old stock (?), pre-1931, 14" by 30".

$425+

Champion Spark Plugs
embossed single-sided tin sign, early design, very good condition, light staining, 5 1/2" by 15".

$400+

Chevrolet
OK Used Cars neon sign, new old stock, 40" tall without post.

$6,000+

Chevrolet
OK Chevrolet Used Cars Authorized Dealer double-sided porcelain sign, very good condition, four quarter-size touchups in field, also touchups to "bull nose" ends, small non-neon version, 42" by 48".

$4,500+

Chevrolet
"bowtie" large single-sided porcelain sign with top flange, near mint, part of large OK Used Car sign, 6" by 17".

$500+

Chevrolet
"bowtie" small single-sided porcelain sign with top flange, excellent condition, chip along edge, part of small OK Used Car sign, 4" by 12".

$500+

Chevrolet
Super Chevrolet Service double-sided porcelain sign, near mint, chip in field, 42" by 48".

$6,750+

Cincinnati Street Railway
original decal on metal, good condition, light staining and small scratches, 20" by 22".

$450+

Cincinnati Street Railway
hat badges, one excellent, one fair to good condition.

$110+ pair

Clayton Dynamometer
die-cut porcelain flange, display side good condition, reverse fair to good with edge chips, 22" by 18".

$2,200+

Clean Comfort Station
single-sided tin sign, excellent condition, 20" diameter.

$400+

Cushman Motor Vehicles
Sales-Service single-sided porcelain sign, good condition, chips at mounting holes, 10" by 12".

$350+

Delco Battery
figural tin display with original box, near mint, 10" by 14" by 8".

$500+

Daimon
(German Battery) single-sided porcelain dome sign, very good to excellent condition, large chip at top mounting hole, 19" by 25".

$250+

We Sell Diamond Squeegee Tread Tires
die-cut tin flange sign, excellent condition, light wear and scratches, 13 1/2" by 18".

$3,250+

Diamond Tires
on sale here double-sided porcelain sign, near mint, 15" by 22".

$4,000+

Dreadnaught Claw Tire Chains
double-sided tin rack top with brackets, good condition, light wear and scratches, 10" by 24".

$600+

Dunlop Tire
mermaid single-sided tin sign, near mint, 19"
by 6".

$5,600+

Edison Mazda Lamps
single-sided tin sign, cardboard back, dated 1923, excellent
to near mint condition, slight wave in upper right corner, 22"
by 11".

$1,500+

Edwards Lakes to Sea System
die-cut cardboard sign, excellent condition, framed, 20" by 28".

$300+

Eveready Daylo
glass counter top show case, with mirrored back, good condition, 12" by 20"
by 12".

$200+

Farmers Automobile Insurance
license plate tag with 1930s car, near mint.

$175+

Eveready Battery
(with boy) single-sided porcelain sign, excellent condition,
slightly bowed, 38" by 17".

$475+

Federal Tires
Authorized Sales Agency single-sided porcelain sign, excellent condition,
some edge chipping, glossy, 18" by 36".

$300+

Firestone
die-cut tire porcelain flange, excellent condition, small
chips around edge and flange, 36" by 28".

$3,500+

Firestone Tires Badge
rubber and celluloid.

$75+

Firestone Tires Garage-Gasoline
die-cut porcelain flange, very good condition, some wear and small chips on edge, porcelain missing from most of flange, 16" by 21".

$800+

Firestone Tires
die-cut double-sided porcelain sign, silver-dollar-size chip along top edge, light scratches in field, 30" by 36".

$1,050+

Fisk Tires
Gasoline Auto Supplies porcelain flange sign, excellent condition, some edge chips, 18" by 24".

$700+

Fisk Time To Re-Tire
molded rubber (?) plaque, near mint, 21" by 14".

$500+

Flippin Parnell Garage
embossed tin license plate tag, excellent condition.

$40+

Ford Lubrication
neon sign.

$3,000+

Ford Service neon sign
excellent condition.

$4,000

Oakland Raiders quarterback Rich Gannon and some of his favorite signs, including a large circa 1953
Ford V-8 single-sided tin sign. They are on display in Gannon's storage facility in suburban Minneapolis.

Francisco Auto Heater
self-framed single-sided tin sign, near mint, light scratches on frame, 18" by 40".

$3,300+

General Tire
neon sign, circa 1939, neon and can replaced.

$2,000+

Gannon's Service
A full-size Gulf gas station, complete with pumps, signs, working restroom, counter with cash register, maps and ephemera, has been built inside quarterback Rich Gannon's storage facility in suburban Minneapolis.

Gillette Tire Bear
die-cut cardboard counter displays with easel backs, very good to
excellent condition, 14" to 19" tall.

$700+ set

Genuine Ford Parts Used Here
single-sided porcelain sign, fair condition, minor chipping, faded, 10" by 25".

$600+

Goodrich Silvertowns
die-cut porcelain flange, excellent condition, some edge chipping, 19" by 23".

$500+

Goodrich Tires Garage
die-cut porcelain sign, near mint, 18" by 18".

$1,600+

Goodyear Service Station
tin flange sign, near mint, 12" by 21 1/2".

$600+

Goodyear Service Station
die-cut porcelain flange sign, near mint, 30" by 26".

$4,750+

Good Year Winged Shoe
porcelain sign, excellent condition, part of larger sign, 6" by 18".

$700+

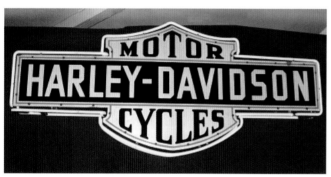

Harley-Davidson Motorcycles
double-sided porcelain sign with neon, overall excellent condition, two chips and light staining, 24" by 60" by 6".

$41,000+

Harley-Davidson Motorcycles
Sales and Service tin flange sign, excellent condition, light scratches, glossy, rare.

$2,250+

Greyhound Package Express
single-sided tin sign, near mint, 18" by 28".

$125+

Harley-Davidson Oil
counter top bookrack, NIB, 11" by 24" by 10".

$900+

Harrelson Rubber Company
tin sign, excellent condition, 10" by 10 1/2".

$75+

Hood Tires
single-sided tin two-piece sign in wood frame, fair condition, wear and staining, 19" by 72".

$375+

Hood Tires Man
tin die-cut metal display rack, early design, good condition, worn, 11" by 15".

$350+

Hood Tires Man
with bowtie license plate tag, poor to fair condition, two nail holes and chip.

$175+

A. E. MEECH, HDW.
DANIELSON, CONN.
NEIGHBORHOOD TIRE EXPERTS
HOOD TIRES

Hood Tires
single-sided tin sign with wooden frame, excellent condition, 12" by 24".

$950+

Ask the "WHY" Of the EXTRA PLY
At This Sign
HOOD TIRES

Hood Tires
single-sided tin sign, early design, good condition, scratches in field, 11" by 17".

$700+

HOOD TIRES

Hood Tires
double-sided porcelain sign, minor touchups, 35 3/4" by 32".

$900+

Hood Tires
single-sided porcelain sign, near mint, 34" by 18".
$1,800+

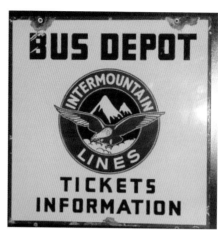

Intermountain Lines Bus Depot
Tickets Information double-sided porcelain sign, good condition in field, large chips around mounting holes, 24" square.
$1,400+

Jefferson Lines Bus Depot
double-sided tin sign, excellent condition, minor edge wear, 24" by 29".
$1,400+

Jefferson Lines
enameled die-cut hat badge, excellent condition.
$100+

Kelly-Springfield
Hand Made Tires & Tubes single-sided tin embossed sign, excellent condition, light waves, framed, 15" by 22".
$3,700+

Kelly-Springfield
single-sided tin sign, excellent condition, light scratches in field, 24" by 16".

$4,000+

Kelly-Springfield
Keep Smiling tin tire display, very good condition, one long scratch in field, light wear, 8 1/2" by 16".

$1,100+

Klaxon Please Drive Slowly
single-sided porcelain sign, United Motor Service, fair to good condition, significant edge chipping and in field, 7 1/2" by 20".

$350+

Kem Ignition-Fuel Pump
reverse-painted lighted counter display, fair to good condition, paint loss and touched up areas, 12" by 18".

$350+

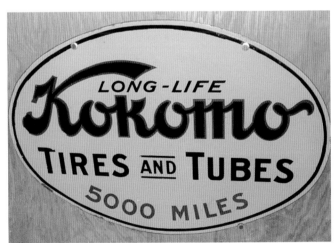

Kokomo Tires and Tubes
double-sided porcelain sign, excellent condition-plus, small chips around edge, 16" by 24".

$1,200+

LaFayette/Nash
two-piece double-sided porcelain sign.

$3,000+

Los Angles TRONA Depot Stages
porcelain flange, excellent condition, with one chip in field on each side, 15" by 16".

$800+

Mapco Speedway Coils
single-sided tin beveled-edge embossed sign, excellent condition, minor paint loss in lower corner, 13" by 9".

$2,500+

Mazda Automobile Lamps
Sold Here porcelain flange sign, near mint, 11" by 15".

$2,700+

Mohawk Tires
painted metal sign, excellent condition, two small scratches at edge of field, 18" by 60".

$2,300+

Moscow, Idaho, OK Rubber Welders
tin license plate tag, fair condition, wear and extra hole.

$40+

Mustang Tires
and Batteries clock, 15" square.

$200+

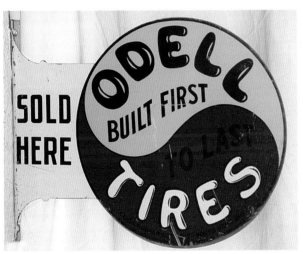

Odell Tires
die-cut porcelain flange, good condition, with wear and scratches, 13" by 18".

$700+

Nealco Anti-Freeze
die-cut license plate tag, excellent condition.

$100+

Niehoff Automotive Products
reverse-painted backlit counter display, excellent condition, 11 1/2" diameter.

$125+

Northland Greyhound Bus Depot
double-sided porcelain die-cut sign, good condition, touched up around mounting holes and edges, minor wear, 20" by 30".

$3,600+

Pacific Piston Rings
double-sided porcelain sign, excellent condition, small edge chips, 16" by 24".

$2,300+

Pacific Trailways Bus Depot
double-sided porcelain sign, excellent condition, chipping around mounting hole, 14" by 24".

$800+

Packard Cables & Terminals
tool tin box, good condition, small dents, 9" by 16" by 10", with cardboard cable box.

$50+

Packard
double-sided porcelain sign, 42" diameter; (Collector Tip: Smaller versions of the Packard sign have been widely reproduced.)

$1,700+

Pay Toilet Seat of Safety
single-sided porcelain sign, near mint, 7" by 3 1/2".

$475+

Perrine Batteries
Polar Bear embossed single-sided tin sign, near mint, 14" by 19 1/2".

$325+

Pomona Bus Lines
single-sided porcelain sign, very good condition, dime-size chip in outer ring, edge chips, 15" by 27".

$650+

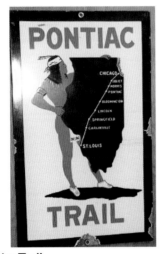

Pontiac Trail
(Pre-Route 66) single-sided porcelain sign, good condition, small area of crazing, chips around edge, 23" by 14".

$5,750+

Pullman Tires
porcelain flange, excellent condition, 17" by 14".

$550+

Railway Express Agency
single-sided tin cardboard-backed sign, good condition, light wear along right edge, 13" by 19".

$600+

Rival Auto Lamps
Made in England cardboard display with 12 lamps, 7 1/2" by 7".

$225+ all

Saxon Motor Cars
double-sided porcelain sign, circa 1920, edge chips, 18" square.

$3,000

Saxon Motor Car Co., Detroit and Ypsilanti, Mich. The Saxon appeared in the winter of 1913-14 as a small two-seater roadster with a 1.4-liter four-cylinder engine, and a two-speed rear-axle gearbox, soon replaced by a three-speed unit. Electric lights were available at extra cost. At $395, these wire-wheeled cars caught the public fancy and although they looked more like cycle cars than conventional small automobiles, sales were high from the first. Peak year was 1916, with 27,800 delivered. Continental and Ferro engines were used and after several thousand Saxons had been sold, wooden artillery spoke wheels were available as an option. Various improvements were noted through 1915 and a small number of delivery vans were produced to augment the roadster in the Saxon range. By 1915, electric lighting was standard equipment. A 2.9-liter six-cylinder touring car still with rear-axle gearbox appeared in 1915 as a companion to the four-cylinder roadsters, which were retained until 1917, when Saxon reached 10th place in sales among American manufacturers. In 1920, a four-cylinder overhead-valve car reappeared and by 1921, sixes were discontinued. In the years following this reappearance, the Saxon models were known as Saxon-Duplex. Production dropped rapidly; the last cars were sold early in 1923. Source: The New Encyclopedia of Automobiles, 1885 To The Present

Schrader Air Service
Kit for the Farm, excellent condition, 3" by 8" by 8".

$375+

Seiberling Steel Radial Tire
clock (clock by Sessions), working condition.

$50+

Simoniz Your Car
reverse-painted, backlit light, excellent condition, 10" by 22".

$200+

Simoniz
cardboard counter display with three cans, near mint, 12" by 16" by 10".

$450+

Solano County Road Commission
single-sided porcelain sign, quarter-size chip around
mounting hole, 12" diameter.

$650+

Sorensen Ignition
wall mount parts rack, excellent condition, 1/2" by 12".

$80+

Southland Greyhound
double-sided porcelain sign, restored, 30" by 25".

$2,500+

Sterling Ignition Cables
neon sign, excellent condition, 12" by 26".

$2,100+

Sportsman Park
Bedford, Ohio, Midget Auto Racing tin license plate tag, near mint.

$200+

Thoma Glass
Authorized Sales & Service double-sided porcelain die-cut sign, excellent
condition, dime-size chip along upper edge, quarter-size chip on reverse, 22"
by 30".

$3,250+

Timken Bearings
neon display sign, 12" by 21".

$500+

Timken Bearings
lighted counter display, near mint, 9" by 16".

$400+

The Union Ice Company
single-sided porcelain sign, good condition, large
chips around mounting holes, 36" diameter.

$3,100+

Union Pacific Stages
North Western Bus Depot double-sided
porcelain sign, near mint, 33" by 26".

$2,500+

U.S. Royal Cord Tires
die-cut flange sign, very good condition, light
scratches, 31" by 24".

$1,800+

United Motors Service
double-sided porcelain sign.

$3,000+

Victor Gasket
girlie print by Medcalf, 20" by 16".

$140+

Vitalic Tires
Bicycles-Motor Cycles single-sided tin sign, embossed treads, excellent condition, slight wave, 12" by 16".

$500+

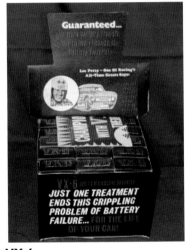

VX-6
battery additive cardboard display, with 15 boxes.

$45+

Wagner Comax Brake Lining
reverse-painted backlit counter display, good condition, some paint loss at top and lower left, 10 1/2" by 17 1/2".

$125+

Wareco Willey
neon sign, excellent condition, 20" by 19".

$675+

Washington Chief
tin license plate tag, near mint condition.

$325+

Weed Chains
tin gasoline price sign, good condition, wear, fading and scratches, 23" by 17".
$400+

Westinghouse Mazda Lamps
reverse-painted backlit counter display, excellent condition, 10" by 16 1/2".
$400+

White Trucks-Busses
Indiana Trucks double-sided porcelain sign, near mint,
20 1/2" by 27".

$3,000+

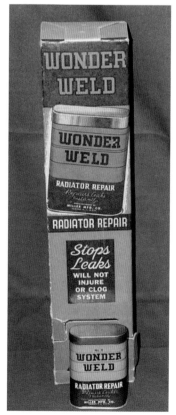

Wonder Weld Radiator Repair
cardboard display, full, 14" by 3".
$50+

X Liquid Repairs
Leaky Radiators chalkboard single-sided tin embossed
sign, excellent condition, light wear, 27" by 20".
$1,100+

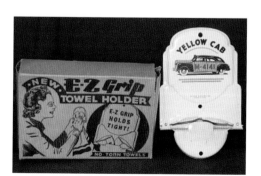

Yellow Cab
Towel Holder and original box, excellent condition.
$130+